Faith Simplified

Faith Simplified

Knowing What You Believe
So You Can Believe It Better

Carol Peterson

edited by
Don Bertelsen and Jim Peterson

RESOURCE *Publications* · Eugene, Oregon

FAITH SIMPLIFIED
Knowing What You Believe So You Can Believe It Better

Copyright © 2022 Carol Peterson. All rights reserved. Except for brief quotations in critical publications or reviews, no part of this book may be reproduced in any manner without prior written permission from the publisher. Write: Permissions, Wipf and Stock Publishers, 199 W. 8th Ave., Suite 3, Eugene, OR 97401.

Resource Publications
An Imprint of Wipf and Stock Publishers
199 W. 8th Ave., Suite 3
Eugene, OR 97401

www.wipfandstock.com

PAPERBACK ISBN: 978-1-6667-4465-1
HARDCOVER ISBN: 978-1-6667-4466-8
EBOOK ISBN: 978-1-6667-4467-5

JULY 27, 2022 10:19 AM

All Scripture quotations, unless otherwise indicated, are taken from the Holy Bible, New International Version®, NIV®. Copyright ©1973, 1978, 1984, 2011 by Biblica, Inc.™ Used by permission of Zondervan. All rights reserved worldwide. www.zondervan.com. The "NIV" and "New International Version" are trademarks registered in the United States Patent and Trademark Office by Biblica, Inc.™

Scripture quotations marked English Standard Version (ESV) are from the Holy Bible, English Standard Version, copyright © 2001 by Crossway, a publishing ministry of Good News Publishers. Used by permission. All rights reserved.

Scripture taken from the Holy Bible: International Standard Version® Release 2.0. Copyright © 1996-2013 by the ISV Foundation. Used by permission of Davidson Press, LLC. ALL RIGHTS RESERVED INTERNATIONALLY.

Scripture quotations marked King James Version (KJV) are taken from the Holy Bible, King James Version (Public Domain).

Scripture quotations marked New Living Translation (NLT) are taken from the Holy Bible, New Living Translation, copyright ©1996, 2004, 2015 by Tyndale House Foundation. Used by permission of Tyndale House Publishers, Carol Stream, Illinois 60188. All rights reserved.

Some content taken from *Tyndale Bible Dictionary* by Philip W. Comfort, PhD. Walter A. Elwell, PhD, eds. Copyright © 2001. Used by permission of Tyndale House Publishers. All rights reserved.

This book is dedicated to every Christian who seeks greater understanding of their faith but who needs a place to begin that quest, and to people trying to see what Christianity is all about and how they fit in with God's plan.

It is also dedicated to our family members and friends who have encouraged us in our faith and throughout this project. Thank you.

Always be prepared to give an answer to everyone who asks you to give the reason for the hope that you have.

1 Peter 3:15

Contents

Introduction | ix

1. I Already Believe in Jesus, So What's in This Book for Me? | 1
2. The Father's Plan | 13
3. What About Trust? | 24
4. We Need Saving | 45
5. How Did Jesus Change Things? | 56
6. Commandments One Through Three | 69
7. Commandment Four | 77
8. The Final Six Commandments | 82
9. The 613 Were God's Laws, Too | 98
10. Jesus Fulfilled the Law | 111
11. God Simplified the Law into Two Rules | 126
12. Love God with All Your Heart, Soul, Mind, and Strength | 131
13. How Do I Love Others as Myself? | 147
14. The Gift of Judgment | 159
15. Discernment | 167
16. Free Will | 177
17. Our Most Important Free Will Choice | 189
18. Simplifying Our Faith | 192

Appendix A
    The Apostles' Creed | 201

Appendix B
    Discussion of *Praus* (*Meek*) in Horse Training | 203

Appendix C
    God's Plan | 204

Appendix D
    God's Promises | 206

Appendix E
    Do People Go to Heaven if They Have Never Heard About Jesus? | 207

Appendix F
    Why Did God Select the Levites as Priests? | 209

Appendix G
    Works v. Grace | 210

Appendix H
    Blasphemy | 212

Appendix I
    Baptism | 214

Appendix J
    The Roman Road to Salvation | 216

Bibliography | 219

Introduction

GOD WANTS IT SIMPLE for us to have faith. He also gave us minds so we can have clarity about what our faith is based on. When asked what the basis of Christianity is though, Christians often simply respond, "Jesus died to save us" or "it is based on the Bible." They don't know where in the Bible the theology of salvation originated or why it makes sense to believe it. Without that clear understanding, it is hard to explain Christianity to others. It is hard to explain it to ourselves.

Many Christians claim Christian beliefs while being vague on what those are and why they say they believe them. That doesn't mean they are not Christian. Faith in what Jesus did is the only thing required for our salvation. But understanding the theology of salvation as spread throughout the entire Old and New Testaments helps deepen a person's faith because we see the logical progression of God's plan. Phrases we hear bandied about at church finally make sense in the context of God's plan. When we hear them; when we say them ourselves, they finally have meaning.

When our faith has meaning inside our heads in addition to inside our hearts, our faith is more powerful, more exciting, more meaningful—even for folks who don't have a degree in theology. To clarify Christianity for non-theologians, is why we project team members joined together to create this book.

Carol Peterson was raised in a Christian home, the daughter of a United Methodist minister. As an adult, she attended many varieties of churches, including Lutheran, Pentecostal, non-denominational evangelical, and Church of God. Growing up though, she had no clue what the principles of Christianity were and why she should believe them. Nor did she even know what questions to ask. In-depth Bible study (as a participant, leader, and writer of studies) clarified aspects of Christianity, but she still struggled to pull them together and see them as a whole.

Introduction

Pastor Don Bertelsen was raised in a non-practicing Christian family. He sporadically attended a variety of Christian churches, when invited by friends. The Christian influence from his parents came both from protestant and Roman Catholic backgrounds, but he grew up not knowing what he should believe or why. As an adult, he pursued an understanding of those beliefs, graduating from Mid America Christian University with a degree in Pastoral Ministries.

Pastor Don was ordained as a minister in the Church of God and began his pastoral career in 1986, serving as lead pastor for over 30 years. He is the theological check for the project team, to make sure non-mainstream thinking stays out of the mix. He is also uniquely able to see how the Old and New Testaments make sense when viewed together, while the rest of us are still stumbling over those tongue-tying names!

Jim Peterson has led in-depth Bible studies for years. Like the other members of the team, Jim loves digging in to understand God's plan in more detail and then sharing that understanding. He was raised in a Roman Catholic home and attended parochial school. He also grew up not knowing what he should believe or why. As an adult, he attended the same churches as Carol, who, not coincidentally, is his wife.

The initial idea for this book originated with Jim. A big skill Jim brings to the project team is an ability to ask probing questions that cause the rest of the team to search Scripture for answers. Jim figures that if there is something in the Bible that makes a person scratch his head, it is not the Bible's fault. The Bible should make sense. It is God's word, after all. Therefore, us mortals are missing something. Fortunately, Jim is also a degreed engineer which helps him look at the Bible with the same analytical view he used in his career. It isn't enough to understand parts of theology individually. Jim seeks to understand how those parts work together as a whole.

All of the project team members have participated in many varieties of Christianity. Doctrines among denominations may vary slightly. Rules of conduct can be different. But they all are based on one thing: Divine Jesus, the Son of God, became the blood sacrifice that has the power to forgive our sins, make us right in God the Father's eyes, and allow our souls to spend eternity in Heaven with him. Resurrection was the proof Jesus gave us to show his power over death.

That is the basis of Christianity. The "how that works" is the basis of this book. While salvation is attained solely on a belief in Jesus, faith is usually stronger when we understand why that belief is warranted. Our goal

Introduction

is that you will see how the theology of Christianity makes perfect sense. Our prayer is that your faith will be stronger because of that understanding.

1

I Already Believe in Jesus, So What's in This Book for Me?

As a kid, I spent every Sunday morning at church. I even listened to the sermons. Dad was the pastor so I knew we'd be talking about the sermon over dinner. I grew up hearing terms like *salvation, righteousness, sacrifice*. But there was something missing. I didn't actually know what those words meant, why they were important, or why I should believe them. They didn't make sense to me.

As an adult, I asked people in our Bible study to pray for me as I set out to understand why God required the ancient Israelites to perform all those messy blood sacrifices. One of our group members reacted by telling me that I don't need to understand because Jesus took care of the sacrifice for me. What he said was absolutely true.

My faith is stronger, however, if I understand what I say I believe. If Jesus became the blood sacrifice to forgive my sins, I wanted to know why God the Father needed a blood sacrifice at all. And why Jesus was the only one who could be that sacrifice. To understand what I—as a Christian—claim I believe, I wanted to understand where those ideas came from and what they mean for me. So, I proceeded with the study.

Troubling Numbers

Evidently, I wasn't alone in not understanding what I say I believe as a Christian. A full 60 percent of Christians participating in the 2020 Lifeway

Research Survey believed that "everyone eventually goes to heaven."[1] Eternal life whether or not Jesus is involved? That's not part of our Christian beliefs.

Also in that Lifeway survey, 65 percent of Christians polled said they believed "smallest sins" do not warrant eternal damnation.[2] Any unforgiven sin that is OK with God? That's not part of our Christian beliefs.

In the 2020 American Worldview Inventory (AWI), 48 percent of the Christians polled, believe they must do good works to gain God's acceptance.[3] Earning salvation by what we do? That's not part of our Christian beliefs.

The AWI survey also showed over 50 percent of Christians believe "there is no absolute moral truth," and that right and wrong is determined by factors other than the Bible.[4] A majority of Christians surveyed said that "the Bible is not the authoritative and true word of God." No moral truth? The Bible not the true word of God? That's not part of our Christian beliefs.

The AWI survey also reported that 62 percent of self-described Christians surveyed believed that simply having faith—whether it is Buddhism, Hinduism, Islam or Christianity, matters more than which faith you have.[5] Any worship other than God the Father, Son, and Holy Spirit? That's not part of our Christian beliefs.

Despite or perhaps because of these misconceptions about Christianity, 75 percent of the Ligonier Ministries survey takers agreed that learning about theology is not just for pastors and scholars.[6] In other words, theology is something all Christians should study. The problem evidently is that no one is teaching it. Or not teaching it in a way that is simplified and understandable.

Clearly, many Christians do not know the basic principles of Christianity. Clearly, many Christians do not recognize what those principles are based on. Clearly, many Christians do not understand what they say they believe. That does not mean those people are not Christian. But it points out an undeniable need for Christians to know what Christianity means. An added benefit of knowing is that the result is almost always deeper faith.

1. Ligonier.org., *Lifeway Survey White Paper*, 4
2. Ligonier.org., *Lifeway Survey White Paper*, 12
3. ArizonaChristian.edu., American Worldview Inventory Results, 3
4. ArizonaChristian.edu., American Worldview Inventory Results, 2–4
5. ArizonaChristian.edu., American Worldview Inventory Results, 2
6. Ligonier.org., *State of Theology Survey Highlights*, 19

Over the years, members of the project team for this book have asked other Christians to explain Christian points they claim they believe. They can't. We have asked them to at least say what those beliefs are based on. "The Bible," they say, but don't know where in the Bible it talks about those beliefs. Or they say, "I heard it in church," but don't know where the pastor got that idea either.

When we briefly explain to those same Christians a term they have heard but didn't understand, showing where it came from in Scripture and how it relates to other passages in the Bible, the first response is almost always surprise. Then the person responds, "That makes so much sense!" Then comes excitement. There is understanding. There is belief. There is renewed enthusiasm for their faith as they recognize how Christianity is founded on something solid and rational. Suddenly, Christianity no longer feels like it is based on bits of Scripture quoted at random. It now makes common sense.

Good news! It will make sense to you, too.

Questions you may have

You have heard that God loves us unconditionally. Do you know what that means or where that idea stems from? How can we say God loves us but then allows bad things to happen? How can God love us but then send all those people to Hell?

Most of us at one time have reached a point of despair, needing to trust God. How can we trust Almighty God to care about our personal needs? Isn't he too busy keeping the universe going?

Is the God of the Old Testament even the same God of the New Testament? And why should we bother reading the Old Testament? Didn't Jesus make the Old Testament irrelevant?

We know God wants us to love him but what does that mean? Sometimes we don't feel capable of loving him. How can we love God when we do not have an emotional response to him?

What does it mean that we receive the Holy Spirit when we believe in Jesus? Why would the Holy Spirit want to live in us? Is there a purpose other than to guide our earthly lives?

We make many decisions each day. How do even small decisions have huge consequences in our earthly life? How do they affect our eternal life?

To help answer those questions and to clarify what we, as Christians believe, what those beliefs are based on, and why it makes sense to believe them, this book asks the following questions.

1. Just what is God's plan, and can we trust him?

    You have been told that God is trustworthy. This book will establish God's trustworthiness based on his character and what he has done. You will learn how God was not only trustworthy throughout biblical times, but how he is also trustworthy in your life today. You will understand that God had a plan of salvation from the beginning when he first created the world and placed mankind in it. By the end of this book, you will be able to explain God's plan to others, recognize how it was his plan from the beginning, and how he has simplified our part in that plan.

2. If God is so good and trustworthy, why do we need a Savior?

    Does God let everyone into Heaven or is eternal life conditional on something he has planned? You will see why we need a Savior and will have an answer to that bothersome question about why Jesus had to die for our salvation. By the end of this book, you will be able to explain to others what this means and how it is a way God has simplified our part in his plan.

3. If God planned to save us anyway, why did he make all those rules?

    What do you think? Did he do it for our salvation? To force us to do what he wanted? To make himself look more important? We will look at the Ten Commandments in a new and vibrant way that will change your view of them. By the end of the book, you will understand the simplicity of those ten and the other laws God dictated to Moses, and recognize how God gave them to us, not for our salvation, but to make our lives better.

4. What does it mean that "Jesus fulfilled the law?" Whatever did Jesus have to do with those rules?

    Does fulfilling the law mean we don't have to follow God's rules anymore? We will see how Jesus did not get rid of those laws, but took care of them for us by what he did and then consolidated them into just two. By the end of this book, you will be able to explain to others what "fulfilling the law" means and how Jesus further simplified our part in God's plan.

5. How are judgment and free will God's dangerous gifts?

   Remember that Lifeway survey? A whopping 65 percent of people surveyed believe that a person's "smallest sins" will not keep them out of Heaven. They are right. But there is fine print involved. Do you know what that fine print says, why it is there, and why it is significant?

   We will look at God's gift about judgment and understand what it means that the Father looks at our hearts for evidence of our surrender to Jesus. We will also see how one of God's gifts to us—free will—is the one with the greatest and potentially most dangerous current and eternal consequences. By the end of this book, you will be able to explain judgment and free will to others and how they are a way God has simplified our part in his plan.

   Using those five questions as a guide, we will

- Start with Genesis and explore God's plan of salvation throughout Scripture
- Establish that God is trustworthy
- Discuss the ancient Jewish sacrificial system that covered sins
- Explore how Jesus became the blood sacrifice to not only cover sins but forgive them
- Delve into the Ten Commandments and see how each one benefits our life here on earth before we ever get to perfect Heaven
- Look at the laws of Moses as the way God simplified life for his nomadic people
- See how Jesus fulfilled the law relating to priesthood, the Temple, the sacrificial system, and daily life
- Understand how Jesus also fulfilled the writing of the ancient prophets as to the new thing God was doing
- Plunge into Jesus' two greatest commandments, recognize where in Scripture they first appeared, and how we are to love with our heart, soul, mind, and strength

- Address the types of biblical love set out in Scripture and what they mean, as to loving God and others
- Explore our duty to leave judgment to God but have discernment in life
- Recognize how our exercise of free will comes with consequences; especially our free will choice about Jesus

Looking at all those topics you will see how they work together. You will see how throughout it all, God has simplified our part in his plan. You will see the logic and common sense behind his plan.

We are one church

Many churches recite *The Apostles' Creed* as part of their service. Maybe you recite *The Apostles' Creed* in your church, too or maybe you've never heard of it. It sets out what the early church believed, based on the teachings of Jesus' remaining eleven disciples who learned directly from him. It nicely summarizes Christian theology. You can read *The Apostles' Creed* in full (Appendix A), but here are its points:

- We believe in the Trinity—God the Father, God the Son, and God the Holy Spirit as equal persons.
- We believe Jesus is inseparably fully human and fully God, being born of a virgin woman and conceived by the Holy Spirit.
- Jesus suffered, was crucified, died, and was buried. He rose from the dead and went to Heaven where he sits on the throne with God the Father, judging all people.
- We believe in Christ's universal, eternal church, which includes all believers, living and dead.
- We believe Jesus has the power to forgive our sins. Because of our belief in him and resulting forgiveness, when we die, we will live eternally in Heaven.

That's it.

If your church does not recite *The Apostles' Creed*, have you read your church's statement of faith? It is usually somewhere easy to find, often on the church's website. Do you understand what that statement of faith says?

Do you understand why it says what it says? Can you explain each point to someone else? Are there points in your church's statement of faith that are in addition to the ones listed above?

Additions in a church's or denomination's statement of faith do not necessarily mean that church or denomination is not Christian. Nor does it mean that church or denomination is *more Christian* than others. Rather those additions are generally there as an expression of their faith; not elements required for salvation.

The focus of *Faith Simplified*, therefore, is to look only at what all Christians believe. Scripture makes more logical, rational sense when looked at without doctrines that are not related to salvation and which may vary from denomination to denomination. It helps us see God's hand at work in a steady, continuous fashion. His plan becomes uncluttered and apparent. Moreover, we can see how he has simplified our part in that plan.

Members of the project team have come from a wide variety of denominational backgrounds. We have loved them all. We therefore have no agenda to push when it comes to denominational preference. We will focus only on what all Christians believe. Are you relieved?

But theology is scary

Theology is a big, confusing word. You might wonder: if I am to understand theology, don't I need a degree from a seminary and have doctorates in philosophy and comparative religions? Surely theology isn't for us regular folks, right?

No. That's not right. Theology is simply a study of God and his relation to the world. That doesn't sound so intimidating. Although God is not completely knowable by us, he graciously leaves indications of his character, his love, and his plan for us in Scripture. Glimpsing those love notes helps us unravel his plan—which itself reveals his character and love for us.

Christian theology attempts to put into words God's plan covering aspects of this life and our eternal life. It encompasses things we can't imagine; questions we don't know to ask. Jesus told us to have faith like a child, inferring it should be simple. While this book will cover several theological issues in detail, the goal is to bring everything back to simple elements.

That is good, because as that 2020 Ligonier's survey showed, most Christians do not believe theology is only for pastors and scholars to study. Theology is for the rest of us, too.

Where did this book come from?

Just how does this book go about summarizing God's massively detailed plan for simpler understanding?

Naturally, the primary research for this book was the Bible. Often, a single verse of Scripture was studied in multiple versions of the Bible to make sure the meaning was clear among all of them, without discrepancy or lack of clarity. What is the same? What is different? Does the difference matter?

Then original Hebrew and Greek words used in specific verses were researched, because often, the meaning of a word changes over time. Our modern definition may mean something quite different from the original word.

For example, Jesus is described in Scripture as *meek*.[7] A modern definition of *meek* implies weakness. "Wait a minute, you say," picturing images of Jesus turning over the Temple tables with his handmade whip. "Weakness doesn't describe divine Jesus, the Son of God, at all. So what is going on?"

The meaning of words change over time

Let's look at the original meaning of *meek*.

For Greater Depth

> Some Bible versions use the English word *humble* instead of *meek*. The original Greek word however translates as *meek* (and the related adjective *meekness*). That original Greek word is *praus*. *Praus* is an adjective that comes from the nouns *prautes* and *praotes*. Both *prautes* and *praotes* refer to gentleness in power or power under control.[8] They also refer to grace of the soul expressed toward God, accepting God's dealings with us as good and not resisting them.[9] The meekness displayed by Jesus is the

---

7. See Matt 11:29; 2 Cor 10:1; see also Matt 5:5 quoting Ps 37:11 about meekness as a godly attribute

8. Vine, *Dictionary*, 401

9. Zodhiates, *Dictionary*, 1208–1210

> fruit of his power. Jesus was *meek* because He had the infinite resources of God at his command.[10]

Jesus came to do the will of the Father and did not avoid doing it.[11] Notice that the original definition above for *meek* includes an element of power. That is nearly the exact opposite of our modern definition of *meek* as *weak*. Let's bring the proper definition into clarity.

A horse is powerful, strong, and intimidating. But when trained, that power is kept under control and used for a specific purpose. Imagine a little girl approaching a massive horse. The horse—though strong and imposing—lets her stroke his nose. That is gentleness in power. The horse later pulls a wagon, plows a field or is ridden by a knight into battle without resisting his master. That is power under control. The horse is *meek*, according to the ancient definition.

In fact, many Bible scholars believe the term *prautes* was used by ancient Greeks specifically to refer to the process of training wild horses, for use in the military. That trained horse would work willingly under the guidance of its master. The horse was powerful, but could keep that power under control, maintaining a calm or gentle nature when needed, even during battle. (See Appendix B for a discussion of the word used in horse training).

A person in Jesus' time would have understood the meaning of *prautes*. It would have made common sense to apply that term to all-powerful Jesus. Knowing the original meaning of the word *meek* better describes Jesus who came to do the Father's will. It does not conflict with our understanding of the character of Jesus, the Son of God. Jesus on earth was not a weak man people could push around. Jesus is the all-powerful creator of the universe. He knew how and when to use his power while on earth to further the purpose for which he came—the will of the Father, which he did willingly, knowing that purpose was good and not disputing or resisting it. He utilized that power while being gentle in spirit. Jesus is not weak. Jesus is powerful.

Another example that illustrates the meaning of *prautes* as meekness is that of a king exercising goodwill and gentleness when he wields his power in the kingdom. That definition also would perfectly describe Jesus, our eternal King.

---

10. Vine, *Dictionary*, 401
11. Matt 26:39, 42; Mark 14:36; John 4:34; 5:19, 30; 6:37–40; 14:31

Jesus, described as meek in Scripture, now makes sense. Did a light bulb suddenly appear over your head? Do you have new insight? Are you excited how defining a single word could so influence your understanding of Scripture?

Defining a specific word by its original meaning in the specific verse of Scripture where it is found helps avoid inaccurate definitions. It makes Scripture more understandable. You will be surprised at how much more sense—and indeed, how much more *common sense*—Scripture makes when you know the original meaning of words used, not how our modern world defines them.

Finally, the project team studied how one verse of Scripture might augment, explain, and support another, between the Old and New Testaments. When we see God's plan being implemented and recorded in both the Old and New Testaments, it not only makes more sense, it also increases our faith because we see God as good and trustworthy since the beginning of everything.

Simple is good

Some aspects of Christianity presented in this book sound complicated until they are unraveled. Some you may have always wondered about. Some you may have never given a thought. But the hope is that a deeper understanding will increase your awe of God's plan and your gratitude that he took his intricate plan and simplified our part in it.

The overriding and underlying purpose of *Faith Simplified* is to realize that theology may seem complicated at first, but it should still make sense. Despite how God made our part in his plan simple, we humans tend to make it complicated. It does not need to be. After presenting basic principles, this book will encourage you to then set the theological explanations up on your spiritual shelf for safe keeping and focus on truth that reflects the Father's character. Therefore, as you read, please remember:

- God wants it to be easy for us to be with him.
- Theology may feel complex but it should still make sense.
- Faith should be simple.

Principle 1

Can We Trust God and His Plan?

2

The Father's Plan

In the beginning, God created the heavens and the earth (Gen 1:1).

God doesn't do haphazard or random. Nor does he create a jumbled mess. Rather, God has a plan, which he carefully and methodically executes. When it came to life on this earth, God first created the heavens—a location in which to place the Earth. Then he created this planet. Then he made light and dark so the living things he had planned could survive. Then he created water *before* he filled it with fish and sea creatures. Then he created dry ground and plants *before* he filled the sky with birds so that they would have a place to rest and find food. Only after the land was covered with everything land creatures needed, he then created those creatures, including man and woman. The plan of creation was complex. It was detailed. Nothing was done before the foundation was laid for the next step.

But God's plan extends beyond just the creation of this world. It is vast and detailed and eternal. The best part of his plan for us is how he has created a way for us to be with him forever.

What we don't understand

We know little about what exists beyond our galaxy. Science seeks to explain what we don't understand in the universe. Sometimes science succeeds; sometimes it fails miserably. Still we seek.

PRINCIPLE 1 | CAN WE TRUST GOD AND HIS PLAN?

We are given glimpses of Heaven by the Apostle John's revelation, but we can't quite imagine the breadth and scope of it. We are told in Scripture that there is a spiritual battle for our souls between Satan and his minions and God and his angels. We are told it is ongoing and surrounds us in the "spiritual realm"—invisible to our human sight.[1] We don't understand what that battle entails or what it looks like, but we do know the battle involves our part in God's plan.

We know from Scripture that God the Father exists, has always existed

> Before the mountains were born or you brought forth the whole world, from everlasting to everlasting you are God.[2]

... and will always exist.

> to the only God our Savior be glory, majesty, power and authority, through Jesus Christ our Lord, before all ages, now and forevermore! Amen.[3]

God the Father has existed from the beginning and will exist forever. But we don't comprehend how that works.

We know that Jesus has also existed from the beginning because the Apostle John tells us that Jesus spoke the universe into existence—according to God the Father's plan.

> In the beginning was the Word [Jesus], and the Word was with God, and the Word was God. He was with God in the beginning.[4]

John reported Jesus confirming his eternal existence.

> "Very truly I tell you," Jesus answered, "before Abraham was born, I am!" (John 8:58)

We know also that the Holy Spirit has existed from the beginning, hovering over the waters at Creation.

> In the beginning God created the heavens and the earth. Now the earth was formless and empty, darkness was over the surface of the deep, and the Spirit of God was hovering over the waters (Gen 1:1–2).

1. See John 10:10; Eph 6:11–12, Col 1:13; Jas 4:7; 1 Pet 5:8; Rev 12:9, 17; 20:1–15, in fact, most of the book of Revelation
2. Ps 90:2; see also Gen 1:1
3. Jude 1:25; see also 2 Tim 1:9; Jer 10:10; Deut 33:27
4. John 1:1–2; explanation added; see also Col 1:15–16

The Father's Plan

We call God's essence of the Father, Son, and Holy Spirit, the Trinity. We try to explain it as one God existing in three forms. But we don't actually understand how that works. In fact, God's plan is so far beyond our understanding that likely we will never understand most of it. But still we try. Scripture tells us that the Father loves that we seek him and try to know him and his plan for us. When we do try to understand, we see clearly that we are part of that plan—both humanity as a whole and each of us individually. Fortunately, glimpsing God's plan is not completely impossible. He has unveiled much of his plan over time through Scripture.

What we do understand

God the Father's creations are perfect and created exactly as planned—even those odd-looking giraffes and artichokes. They are perfect because they were planned with care, detail, and love. His plan itself is also perfect, planned with care, detail, and love. In fact, his plan for us is so perfect that it has not changed since day one of Creation.

> He has saved us and called us to a holy life—not because of anything we have done but because of his own purpose and grace. This grace was given us in Christ Jesus *before the beginning of time* (2 Tim 1:9; emphasis added).

The English Standard Version says it this way:

> [God] who saved us and called us to a holy calling, not because of our works but because of his own purpose and grace, which *he gave us in Christ Jesus before the ages began* (explanation and emphasis added).

God the Father planned a purpose and grace for us through Jesus. He did this before the beginning of time; before the ages began. That plan to give us grace through Jesus has not changed. The Father's character has not changed either. He still loves us enough to want the best for us. He knows that the best for us is to spend eternity with him.

The good news for those of us trying to understand God's plan, is that Scripture gives us a sequential look at how God has revealed his plan for us so far. Ready for the super speedy, compact, and condensed version of God's plan for our salvation? Here it is.

Principle 1 | Can We Trust God and His Plan?

- After God created everything, he gave us knowledge of good and evil to prepare us to live in a world filled with evil. He then made us mortal—the first step in spending eternity with the Father. He also instituted the sacrificial system to cover our sins by sacrificing one of his own creatures.
- God established the Jewish nation into which Jesus was born.
- Jesus became the single blood sacrifice to make us acceptable to join the Father in Heaven forever.
- Our part in God's plan is to accept that offer.

Wow! Just four bullet points to show the logical sequence of how God the Father is proceeding to implement his loving plan for us to be with him forever. Of course, there is more recorded in Scripture than those four bullet points. A lot more. But those points clarify how the Father has been executing his plan for us from the beginning.

The problem for many of us Christians is seeing how it works together. After all, there are thousands of years between one bullet point and the next. How are each of the points connected? How does one point relate and lead logically to another? (For an expanded version of the four bullet points, see Appendix C.)

God the Father completed execution of the salvation part of his plan when Jesus provided the blood sacrifice for our sins. Is there more to his plan? Yes, absolutely. But for our present earthly lives and our eternal heavenly lives, God's creation of a path to salvation has been fully executed. Done. Everything has been prepared. The system is securely in place. Our participation in that plan is now up to us.

How do we participate in the Father's plan?

Humanity is part of God's ongoing plan. Every part of God's plan moved mankind forward throughout history in how we could live eternally with him. He longs for us to be with him.

> And our fellowship is with the Father and with his Son, Jesus Christ (1 John 1:3).

The Father wants our fellowship.

The Father's Plan

For Greater Depth

> The original Greek word used in 1 John 1:3 for *fellowship* is *koinonia*. It means to share in; to participate in. A synonym of *koinonia* referenced in the definition of *koinonia* is *metoche* meaning partnership.[5]

Based on the definitions of the original Greek word, *fellowship* in 1 John 1:3, infers that the Father wants our participation in his plan. He wants us to share in his plan. He wants us to be a junior partner in his plan. And he wants our participation in his plan to include Jesus.

God loves all of his creations. He made the plan available to all of us humans. The way he has created and implemented his plan is for us to be a partner in his plan through Jesus. Only through Jesus. Some people say God is being unfair to exclude people who don't believe in Jesus. Doesn't God the Father love everyone, not just people who follow Christ?

Yes! Absolutely he does. And the way to reach the Father is available to all of mankind. The way God made available is through Jesus.

Remember that question in Chapter 1 that many people ask? If God loves us, why does he send people to Hell? The answer is, God doesn't send anyone to Hell. We are all headed to Hell on our own. As sinners, we cannot be allowed into perfect Heaven. Perfect Heaven would no longer be perfect if sinners were there.

Nonetheless, the Father wants us to be with him in Heaven forever. Therefore, the Father gave us a way out of that certainty of Hell. God loved humanity as a whole and each of us personally so much that he created a way for us to spend eternity in the best, most wonderful, most perfect place God ever created—Heaven with him—by making us acceptable in his eyes by the forgiveness we can have through Jesus.

People may say, "That's not fair," to require us to go through Jesus for salvation. Clearly, it is God's rule, so it is not up to us to determine its fairness. But from our human perspective, we don't want God to be fair on the issue of salvation. If God were fair, we'd all go to Hell—it's what us imperfect sinners deserve. It is where we are headed on our own.

---

5. Zodhiates, *Dictionary*, 873

So celebrate the truth: God is unfair. He doesn't give us what we deserve. We deserve eternity in Hell. God offers us mercy, made possible by Jesus, to escape that fate.

Celebrate the truth: God is unfair. He gives us what we don't deserve. We don't deserve eternal life in Heaven. God offers us grace—forgiveness we don't deserve, made possible by Jesus. That forgiveness makes us acceptable to be in Heaven with holy God.

Let's repeat that. The Father doesn't send anyone to Hell. We are on our way there by the very fact that we are sinners because perfect Heaven would become imperfect if he let us in. God is holy, divine, perfect. We are not, because we are sinful. By forgiving our sins, we are still not holy, divine, or perfect, but we are acceptable—enough that God can allow us into his presence.

> **Connection Point**: What do you think? Does God compare little sins and big ones and bend his rules to let the people with little sins into perfect Heaven? Is God being unfair to have his plan of salvation in place and base it on mercy and grace?

The Father created a way for us to receive his mercy and grace. Jesus shared that part of the Father's plan when he referred to himself as the "way" that leads to eternal life.

> Jesus answered, "I am the way and the truth and the life. No one comes to the Father except through me."[6]

For Greater Depth

> In John 14:6, the original Greek word for *way* is *hodos*. In this specific verse, *hodos* is a figure of speech that names Jesus as the medium (method; means; process) which allows access to God the Father and eternal life.[7]

Jesus also referred to himself as the "narrow gate" which opens to a road leading to God's Kingdom.

---

6. John 14:6; see also Isa 35:8
7. Zodhiates, *Dictionary*, 1026

The Father's Plan

"Enter through the narrow gate. For wide is the gate and broad is the road that leads to destruction, and many enter through it. But small is the gate and narrow the road that leads to life, and only a few find it" (Matt 7:13–14).[8]

The narrow gate—the single way to spend eternity with the Father—is Jesus. Only when we go through the gate by accepting Jesus' gift of salvation do we begin to walk the Narrow Road that leads to God the Father. Jesus modeled how to live. Jesus taught us about the Father's plan and character. Jesus encouraged us to choose the Father's plan. He gave us reasoning and evidence to make our decision easier.

> **To illustrate the point**: You are in the subway station of a big city. Every person who enters the subway gets a ticket. But in this station, there's no charge. The ticket is free. The cost of the ticket has already been paid. In fact, the person who paid for the ticket also owns the ticket machine. So the ticket machine keeps making more free tickets and never runs out. But in order to get onto the subway train, you first have to drop your ticket into the slot in the turnstile. Once you drop it in, the turnstile lock releases and off you go. Destination: Heaven.
>
> Everyone who enters the subway station must get on a train and go somewhere. You get to choose one of two destinations. There is a second turnstile in the subway station. The tickets for that turnstile are also free. Its destination is Hell.

God's narrow gate is open to all of mankind. Going through it, however, must be chosen on purpose by each person. The Narrow Road is also open to all people once they enter the gate. We simply must choose to walk it. Thus, we can choose to live in communion with God or we can choose to live spiritually alone. That decision also decides where we live eternally—in Heaven with the Father or without him in Hell. That is the decision we must make as it relates to Jesus' Narrow Road for mankind.

God's family plan

In the creation of all things, God created us last. Not as an afterthought. Not as a "might as well." God created us last because we were important.

---

8. See also: Luke 13:24; John 10:2, 7, 9; Rev 3:20–21 reference by Jesus as being a door, as opposed to a gate

Principle 1 | Can We Trust God and His Plan?

He didn't just plop us into Creation. He first prepared a place for us and provided everything we would need. Mankind became the pinnacle; the highlight of his master plan of Creation.

The Gospel of John tells us that it was because God so loved the world (specifically the people in the world) that he gave his only son, Jesus, as a blood sacrifice for our sins. Jesus' sacrifice benefited mankind alone, because God the Father wanted to provide a way for us to live in his presence eternally.

In fact, God's plan went a step further. His plan not only allows a way to live in the Father's presence eternally, but to be adopted into his family.[9] When we accept Jesus' gift of salvation, we move from being mere creations of God to becoming children of God. We are brought into his family through the adoption process (Eph 1:5). Just as adoptive parents *choose* the children whom they adopt, so God chooses us as his children. He loves us that much.

Over and over, Scripture reminds us that God the Father is the Judge. God has given us laws and will judge our hearts when we die. Adoption into God's family is a spiritual process of law. The Father offers us kinship through Jesus. When we accept the offer, Father God, as Judge signs the spiritual adoption papers and we become his children. Although God the Father is eternal, he even puts us into his Will. We become heirs to his kingdom.

We become sons and daughters of the King because God the Father *chose* to adopt us. Chosen to be part of the family of the God of the Universe? How awesome is that?

In the earthly adoption process, parents choose which children to adopt and the adoption proceeds legally, regardless of what the children have to say about it. But with our Heavenly Father's adoption process, he chooses to adopt us into his family, but we must also choose to be adopted by him. We make this choice, by first choosing to follow Jesus. Thus, God's adoption of us into his family, is undisputed—God has chosen us, and we have chosen him. God's adoption of us is different from an earthly adoption. It is not just one sided. In adoption into our heavenly family, God chose us and we choose him.

---

9. See John 15:16 God chose us; Rom 8:29 we are predestined and brothers; Gal 3:26 sons and heirs; John 1:12; Rom 8:16-17 called children of God; Rom 8:14-19 children and heirs; 1 John 3:2 God's children; Matt 12:50 people who do the Father's will are Jesus' family; 2 Cor 6:18 God is father and we are his sons and daughters

To illustrate the point: A couple decided to adopt a child. They had so much joy anticipating their child. Through the adoption process, however, one stumbling block after another occurred. At each problem, they were disappointed, but remained excited about their new family member.

When the adoption finally went through they celebrated their new son joining the family. All their family and friends came to a big party. There was blue confetti, blue balloons, and chocolate cake.

It must be similar with God. God has already reached out to each of us and asked us to be part of his family. He already has the adoption papers ready to sign. God must be filled with joy and anticipation as he and angels wait for us to join him in Heaven. Whenever we stumble, each time we move away from God, he must be disappointed. Still, he has expectation and hope. When we finally choose to believe in Jesus—whoosh—the adoption papers are signed, sealed, and recorded in the heavenly Book of Life. God and the angels rejoice. God's family has grown. He has a new adopted child. Even better, when we die, we will join that celebration in Heaven for eternity. Golden confetti. Balloons of all colors that never pop. Angel food cake. What a party it will be!

Scripture tells us that God chose us from the beginning of the world.

> Even before he made the world, God loved us and chose us in Christ to be holy and without fault in his eyes. God decided in advance to adopt us into his own family by bringing us to himself through Jesus Christ. This is what he wanted to do, and it gave him great pleasure (Eph 1:4–5).

Even before God made the world, he loved us. Even before God made the world, he chose to declare us holy if we believe in his Son. Even before God made the world, he decided to adopt us into his family. God wanted to do this. Loving us, planning for us, implementing his plan for us gave him great pleasure.

Connection Point: All people are God's creations and God wants all people to be his children. He loves everyone. How do you feel knowing that God wants us to share in a more intimate relationship with him, as a child he loves deeply and who will love him in return?

PRINCIPLE 1 | CAN WE TRUST GOD AND HIS PLAN?

God's plan is for mankind and for us individually

God the Father chose to offer salvation through Jesus to everyone. He chose to give each of us the gift of free will to accept that offer—*if we decide to do so*. He chose to make each and every one of us a part of his eternal family—*if we accept the family inheritance he offers*. God the Father loves us so much that he wants us to be no longer just one of his creations, but a personally loved child. The Father's plan, however, hinges on one thing: we have to accept his offer.

Salvation through Jesus is offered to all of mankind. But, at the same time, it is offered to each person individually. Just because the Father offers salvation to everyone does not diminish the eternal and precious value salvation is for each one of us. He loves us, both mankind and each person. That's you. That's your neighbor. That's everyone in your family—even Uncle Roy who hasn't stepped near a church in six decades.

Clearly the Father had a plan for us to be with him forever. Clearly God has been implementing that plan since the beginning of the beginning. Clearly spending eternity in a perfect place where evil, pain, and death do not exist, in the presence of the one who created everything, is evidence of God's love for us. And the best part? God not only offers this plan to mankind in general; he offers it to each of us individually.

God's plan for us sounds good. But can we trust him?

Chapter Summary

- **Theology Simplified:** As humans, we see God's plan in a snapshot, with us as the focus. We know he created a way for us to be with him forever—in Heaven, an even better place than the wonderful world he created for us here. We sometimes struggle to understand parts of God's eternal plan, but it culminates in unending joy for his children, when we choose to become an active part of that plan. He has also laid out his plan for us in a logical, sequential fashion, to reassure us that he developed that plan with care.

- **What's it to me?** Do you dip into Scripture haphazardly? Most of us have a few well-loved verses. We have even memorized some of them. But we often don't see what's recorded in the Bible as God's ongoing plan revealed. When we do, we recognize how his plan was created with detail and skill, revealing more about God's character and his love for us.

- **Faith Simplified:** God has a plan for us to live with him eternally in Heaven. That was his plan for us from the beginning.

3

What About Trust?

Trusting what we can't see

"Trust and validate," parents say about raising their children. But true trust doesn't require validation. If your relationships with people are based on "trust and validate," you are only giving someone the benefit of the doubt until that day you find out they are unworthy. Essentially, it is assuming the person's unworthiness, and being pleasantly surprised when they do something worthy.

 We base our ability to trust others on our human experience. Some people we encounter are trustworthy. But not all of them are. Therefore we cannot assume everyone is. The people who have lost our trust (or never had it) skew our view of everyone and affect our ability to trust anyone. We humans therefore must build up trust with each other over time.

 Our frame of reference in our relationship with God is also based on our human experiences. Trusting God is not usually instantaneous. Most of us must first choose to trust him with small things; things we can't handle ourselves, such as our salvation.

 Salvation? That is not a small thing! No, it is not. It is an enormous, eternal, everlasting thing. But since we can't save ourselves, we have no choice but to trust God to do it for us. That leaves our lives, our circumstances, our physical protection to trust to God. So, we start trusting him with small things—this moment; this circumstance. Did he get us through? Did he guide us? Did he make his presence known to us? If so, maybe I will trust God tomorrow with my family's well-being. Or with my job situation.

Or with my health. Or with my finances. Step-by-step, we learn to trust God over time, with more depth.

To illustrate the point: One day, Jesse brought home a large, unexpected bonus check. His wife smiled. "What do you think about tithing on this—since we weren't expecting the money anyway?"

"Here it comes," Jesse said. Jesse knew his wife wanted to tithe on all the money they brought in. But Jesse wasn't ready to commit to 'this God thing,' especially when it came to money. Ten percent was a lot. With the ten percent he could buy that 65-inch TV he'd been eyeing. Or add it to the pot for retirement.

"God wants us to trust him—even in money matters," Jesse's wife said. "In fact, the Bible actually says we can test God about money."[1]

"Test God?" Jesse liked that idea. No way would God respond to how much they gave. He'd be off the hook from future tithing.

In his arrogance, Jesse nodded. "OK. We'll tithe on this bonus and see what happens." He wrote out a check for $1,000, a tithe of his bonus. He sat next to his wife in church, pretending not to notice the offering plate heading his way. But after a gentle elbow in his ribs, and a moment of hesitation, Jesse dropped the check in the offering plate. That's the end of it, Jesse thought, still thinking about that TV.

A week later, Jesse's company sent him a second check for $1,000. The note with it said there had been an error in calculating his bonus. Jesse was shocked. That second check was exactly the amount he had tithed.

"Isn't that interesting?" his wife said. She paused as Jesse continued to stare at the check. "We are going to tithe on that second check, too, right?"

"Uh," Jesse said. "I guess we can keep testing God on this." He made out a check to the church for $100.

Two weeks later, a surprise $100 check arrived from a credit card rewards program. "Hmm," said Jesse. "Has God been paying attention to me?"

---

1. Mal 3:10

So Jesse tithed on the $100. His wife didn't even have to ask. A week later, a rebate check showed up from a set of tires he had bought last month. The check was $10—the tithe on the $100.

"Coincidence?" asked Jesse's wife.

Jesse couldn't help but laugh. "Too coincidental. I gave God the best test I could. It's like God is grinning and saying, 'My son, you can't outgive me.'"

"By the way," Jesse's wife said. "I found this in your jacket pocket." She handed Jesse a crumpled one dollar bill.

We also learn to trust God when we have a crisis in our lives. We find there is nothing we can do to make things better. We can't see a way out. So we turn to God, saying, "I can't do this on my own, God!" When we turn to God, he proves himself faithful.

Come near to God and he will come near to you (Jas 4:8).

God is always near. James however reminds us that sometimes we have to do the coming near to him first. How many of us know people who never gave Jesus a thought until a crisis appeared in their life? Then they turned to God. Maybe it was only out of desperation. Or because there was nowhere else to go. But they did turn to God. And he comforted them. Maybe he even guided them. He might have resolved the crisis. But always, he loved them. And usually, they sensed that love.

Sometimes, however, we don't see God's hand and his trustworthiness until we have lived through an event and can look back on it.

To illustrate the point: Don tells this story.

Our backyard irrigation system is connected with our neighbors' and with all the farmers' crops in our area. In fact, the main pipeline for the entire system runs through all of the neighborhood backyards and each person is responsible for their section of the pipeline. Last spring, that main pipeline broke and flooded our backyard. We immediately called an excavator to fix it.

The day he arrived, it rained. It didn't just sprinkle. It poured. We almost cancelled the project over worry the back hoe would get stuck in the mud. As the big yellow machine trudged through our muddy yard, I asked God, "Why did you send so much rain?"

It continued to rain all that week. Every day I asked God "Why did you send so much rain? Couldn't you have just waited a week?"

Once the project was finished, the answer was clear. Because it had rained so hard that week, none of our neighbors or any of the nearby farmers needed irrigation water. That meant the system could be shut off without affecting anyone else while we worked to fix our problem. There was not a single complaint from the neighbors or the farmers who relied on that water main. Although we did not see it until after we finished the project, God was definitely at work.

Despite our growing trust and faith, how often do we hear about a Christian who is close to death begin to doubt their salvation? Facing mortality on a personal level, many devoted, believing Christians still have doubt, despite years of belief and growing trust in God. We find it hard to have faith in the unseen.

Jesus' disciple Thomas had trouble believing. After Jesus' death and resurrection, Thomas said he would not believe Jesus had returned from the grave unless he saw the nail wounds and put his fingers in them. When Jesus showed up, Thomas believed.

> Then Jesus told him, "Because you have seen me, you have believed; blessed are those who have not seen and yet have believed" (John 20:29).

Jesus acknowledged how hard it is to believe in the unseen. Fortunately, even with our questions and doubts, we can rely on our rational minds to help us trust God the Father. We can look at what God says and what he does. We can look at God's plan and see our lives as part of it. We can recognize God's promises and how he keeps them as recorded in Scripture and seen in our personal lives. We can choose to trust him because the evidence shows that the Father is worthy of our trust.

So, let's look at why trusting the Father is the rational thing to do.

We have examples of people who trusted God

God loved Noah enough to assure Noah's family's safety from the destruction of the flood. Because Noah trusted God, Noah was obedient, even though Noah couldn't understand God's plan of flooding the earth. Rain?

Principle 1 | Can We Trust God and His Plan?

What's that? Noah must have wondered. But God promised Noah that his family members would be safe. And they were.

After the flood, Noah's family began to repopulate the world. Scripture records the history of Noah's sons and their families. It is not until Abraham (a descendant of Noah's son, Shem) that we glimpse God's love for an individual person again when Scripture tells us, Abraham trusted God. We have many other examples in Scripture of people who trusted God. Here's one.

> **To illustrate the point**: Imagine you are Gideon. God comes to you and says "Gideon, I want you to raise an army for me and fight the Midianites."
>
> "God," you say, "I'm not a general. I don't know how to fight or lead an army. I don't know what to do."
>
> "Gideon," God says, "you're my man."
>
> But you're still not convinced. Hey, here's an idea, you think. I'll lay out this lamb's wool and ask God to make it wet and leave the ground around it dry. If he does that, I'll ask him the next day to leave the lamb skin dry and make the ground wet. Yeah, that's a good idea. If he does both of those things, maybe I'll agree to do what he asks.
>
> You do that and he does that. So you reply, "Everything I have asked of you God, you have done. So OK, I will try."
>
> You go throughout the nation and tell people the news. "God has told me to fight the Midianites."
>
> You are skeptical, but lo and behold, you raise an army of 32,000 men. Thirty-two thousand men! "I can do this!" you say. "God, I feel pretty confident that I can win this battle for you."
>
> "You're missing the point, Gideon," says God. "I'll show you. Cut down the size of your army."
>
> Out of 32,000 men, God tells you to send 22,000 home. You think, Wow, only 10,000 men. I hear the Midianite army is really large. I'm not so confident now. But, hey, maybe I can develop a plan. I'll have some men catch the Midianite army from behind. I'll trick them in the front. You nod. "OK, God. Maybe I can still do this."
>
> "You're not getting the point, Gideon," says God. "Send most of your men home. Get that army down to 300."

You wring your hands. "God," you say, "there is no way I can fight this battle with only 300 men."

God looks at you with love. "You finally get the point. There is no way you can win this battle without me."

You fight the battle and conquer the Midianites.

"God," you say, "I understand. I can do nothing without you."

It took time for Gideon to learn to trust God. But when he did, God proved trustworthy, accomplishing what he said he would do in a way that left no doubt about his power. When we read the scriptural accounts of people who loved God, we have examples of how they trusted him. Those examples can help us know we can trust God, too.

It would be a whole lot better if, instead of struggling, instead of facing a crisis alone, instead of relying on other people to share their story of trust with us, we just started out trusting God. God wants us to trust him. The sooner we accept that point, the easier life becomes. But building trust in God is often a slow process.

Here are more people in Scripture who learned to trust God:

- Isaac: God told Isaac not to go into Egypt, but to stay in the land that he promised. God repeated to Isaac his promise made to Abraham about his offspring bringing blessings on all nations.

   > The LORD appeared to Isaac and said, "Do not go down to Egypt; live in the land where I tell you to live. Stay in this land for a while, and I will be with you and will bless you. For to you and your descendants I will give all these lands and will confirm the oath I swore to your father Abraham. I will make your descendants as numerous as the stars in the sky and will give them all these lands, and through your offspring all nations on earth will be blessed [through Joseph opening the storehouse of food and through Jesus], because Abraham obeyed me and did everything I required of him, keeping my commands, my decrees and my instructions" (Gen 26:2–5, explanation added).

- Jacob was chosen to continue the covenant with God. The Lord appeared to him saying he was the God of Abraham and the God of Isaac.

Principle 1 | Can We Trust God and His Plan?

"I am with you and will watch over you wherever you go, and I will bring you back to this land. I will not leave you until I have done what I have promised you" (Gen 28:15).

- Joseph: When seven years of drought arrived in Egypt, "Joseph opened the storehouses" and provided enough food to bring the nation through the famine. His wise strategy and effective implementation of the plan even allowed Egypt to supply grain to the rest of the world during the famine (Gen 41:57). In this case, God's fulfillment of his promise that Abraham's descendants would be a blessing to the world, occurred not only for the benefit of foreign nations, but even through a foreign nation, Egypt. Joseph told his brothers,

  > You intended to harm me, but God intended it for good to accomplish what is now being done, the saving of many lives (Gen 50:20).

- Deborah: God promised victory to her if she led the Israelites in battle. She sent for Barak son of Abinoam from Kedesh in Naphtali and said to him,

  > "The LORD, the God of Israel, commands you: 'Go, take with you ten thousand men of Naphtali and Zebulun and lead them up to Mount Tabor. I will lead Sisera, the commander of Jabin's army, with his chariots and his troops to the Kishon River and give him into your hands'" (Judg 4:6–7; Deborah speaking).

  The Israelite army was victorious.

- Naaman: King Naaman was told by Elisha to wash in the river seven times and be healed. God had promised healing. The power was in God's word attached to the promised cleansing through the Jordan River. It was God's word that made the Jordan River able to heal Naaman (2 Kgs 5:8–10).

- Job: The LORD not only restored Job's fortunes, he restored them to more than Job had initially. God may seem harsh with his children, but his purpose is the restoration and blessing of his people. As Job said, "Though he slay me, yet will I hope in him" (Job 13:15).

- Daniel: God promised Daniel that "everyone who is found written in the book—will be delivered" (Dan 12:1—Daniel reading from Jeremiah 29:10–14 that the captives would be set free).

- Jeremiah: God proclaims through Jeremiah:

  "Call on me and come and pray to me, and I will listen to you. You will seek me and find me when you seek me with all your heart" (Jer 29:12–13).

- Hannah prayed for a child. Eli the High Priest watching Hannah pray, told her, "Go in peace, and may the God of Israel grant you what you have asked of him" (1 Sam 1:17). Because he was Israel's High Priest, Eli had authority to speak on God's behalf. Because he had that authority from God, Hannah knew those words were God's promise. She later gave birth to Samuel and several other children.

- David: The LORD promised David:

  When your days are over and you rest with your ancestors, I will raise up your offspring to succeed you, your own flesh and blood, and I will establish his kingdom. He is the one who will build a house for my Name, and I will establish the throne of his kingdom forever. I will be his father, and he will be my son . . .
  Your house and your kingdom will endure forever before me; your throne will be established forever (2 Sam 7:12–16).

David's son Solomon built the Temple in Jerusalem and David's throne was established through Jesus' birth into David's family lineage.

- Elizabeth and Zechariah: God promised them a son who would prepare the way for the Lord (Luke 1:17). John the Baptist's ministry is described in Matthew 3:1–12 referring to Jesus, the one who comes after John.

- Mary: The angel of the Lord promised her,

  You will conceive and give birth to a son, and you are to call him Jesus. He will be great and will be called the Son of the Most High. The Lord God will give him the throne of his father David, and he will reign over Jacob's descendants forever; his kingdom will never end (Luke 1:31–33).

Principle 1 | Can We Trust God and His Plan?

Mary later gave birth to Jesus.

- Simeon: Simeon had been visited by the Holy Spirit and told that he would not die until he had seen the Lord's Christ (anointed one).

> It had been revealed to him by the Holy Spirit that he would not die before he had seen the Lord's Messiah. Moved by the Spirit, he went into the temple courts. When the parents brought in the child Jesus to do for him what the custom of the law required, Simeon took him in his arms and praised God (Luke 2: 26–28).

Simeon knew that Jesus was the promised Messiah and that God's promise to him had been fulfilled.

- Ezekiel: God told Ezekiel: "I myself will search for my sheep and look after them" (Ezek 34: 11). Jesus referred to himself as the Good Shepherd.

- Lazarus, Mary, and Martha: Lazarus was sick and Jesus was sent for by Mary and Martha (John 11:1–44).

> When he heard this, Jesus said, "This sickness will not end in death. No, it is for God's glory so that God's Son may be glorified through it" (John 11:4).

Then Jesus brought Lazarus to life.

- Saul who became Paul: God explained to Saul how Jesus fulfilled his promise of a Savior.

> From this man's [David's] descendants God has brought to Israel the Savior Jesus, as he promised. Before the coming of Jesus, John preached repentance and baptism to all the people of Israel. As John was completing his work, he said: "Who do you suppose I am? I am not the one you are looking for. But there is one coming after me whose sandals I am not worthy to untie" (Acts 13:23–25; explanation added).

Paul later preached: "We tell you the good news: What God promised our ancestors he has fulfilled for us, their children, by raising up Jesus" (Acts 13:32).

- Eleven of the 12 disciples and we modern day disciples:

The promise of God's presence.

"And surely I am with you always, to the very end of the age."[2]

The promise of the Holy Spirit.

"And I will ask the Father, and he will give you another advocate to help you and be with you forever— the Spirit of truth. The world cannot accept him, because it neither sees him nor knows him. But you know him, for he lives with you and will be in you" (John 14:16-17).

The Bible contains many of God's promises and how they have been fulfilled. The estimate of how many promises are recorded in Scripture ranges from 300 to several thousand, depending on the scholar's interpretation.[3] Let's use the lower 300 figure. Imagine that someone made 300 promises to you and kept every one of them. When he made his 301st promise, would you trust that he would keep it?

God hasn't made 300 promises to *me*, you say. But he has. He has made promises to mankind and you are part of that group. Even better, although the promises were made to everyone, they were also made to you personally.

Some of those promises you can claim personally are:

- God will help you[4]
- God hears your prayers[5]
- God will lead you[6]
- God is faithful[7]
- God will never leave you[8]
- God will give you strength[9]

---

2. Matt 20:28; see also Heb 13:5 quoting Deut 31:6

3. Estimates of the number of God's promises in Scripture vary depending on how they are counted. See Appendix D for more information

4. Isa 41:13

5. Jer 29:12; Jas 1:5; Mark 11:24

6. Prov 3:6; Isa 58:11

7. 2 Tim 2:13; 2 Thess 3:3; Ps 33:4; 119:90; 1 Cor 10:13; 1 John 1:9

8. Deut 31:6

9. Phil 4:13; Isa 40:29-31; 41:10

PRINCIPLE 1 | CAN WE TRUST GOD AND HIS PLAN?

- God will fulfill your needs[10]
- God will keep you safe from evil[11]
- God heals[12]
- God wants the best for you[13]
- God will provide for you[14]
- God promises eternal life to his children[15]

Connection Point: Which of these promises are most impactful to you? How does it feel, knowing that you can take these promises as ones God has made to you personally?

What about the Father's character can we trust?

The Trinity is comprised of God the Father, God the Son, and God the Holy Spirit. All are equal in importance, power, majesty, and worth. We believe in the concept the Trinity because each part of the Trinity is revealed in various parts of the Bible. We may not understand how the Trinity works, but it is clear from Scripture that the Trinity seems to accurately describe the essence of God. In an attempt to understand better, from our human perspective, we could say that each member of the Trinity manages different parts of God's plan. Looking at the character traits and responsibilities of God the Father can help us understand how he is worthy of our trust.

Tynedale House is the publisher of the modern New Living Translation (NLT) of the Bible. Their *Tynedale Bible Dictionary* specifies the aspects of each member of the Trinity this way:

> Scriptures present the Father as the source of creation, the giver of life, and God of all the universe. The Son is depicted as the image of the invisible God, the exact representation of his being and

---

10. Ps 9:18; Phil 4:19; Rom 8:32
11. Ps 37:40; Jas 4:7
12. Ps 147:3; Exod 15:26
13. Ps 145:9; Jas 1:17
14. Matt 6:31–33; 7:9–11; 2 Cor 9:8
15. Matt 25:46; John 3:14–16, 36; 5:24; 6:40, 47; 10:27–28; 11:25–26; 17:3; Rom 2:6–8; 6:22–23; Gal 6:8; 1 Tim 6:12; Titus 1:2; Jude 1:21; 1 John 2:25; 5:11–14

nature, and the Messiah-Redeemer. The Spirit is God in action . . . reaching people.[16]

Based on that description, let's look at how the three parts of the Trinity work together.

God the Father, as "God of all the universe," is the main authority in the Trinity. Authority here does not refer to supremacy. It refers to responsibility. Jesus often said he came to do the will of the Father. God the Father is the main authority in the Trinity.

God the Father is the planner. As the "source of creation," it was God the Father who created the plan. Jesus spoke it into existence. The Holy Spirit inhabits we believers who live in the created world. The Father made the plan for our salvation through Jesus. It was Jesus who completed the plan according to the Father's will, by living, ministering, suffering, and dying as a sacrifice for us. The Holy Spirit then continued working the Father's plan on earth after Jesus' resurrection and return to Heaven, by living in us.

The Father is about justice.

He gave us laws because of his love for us, knowing we needed them to live life well. The Father establishes covenants (agreements, pledges) with people and upholds his end of them. At final judgment, the Father is the source of ultimate forgiveness—based on each person's relationship with Jesus and the presence of the Holy Spirit—the Father's plan from the beginning.

The Father is patient.

Scripture tells us that the Father is patient and slow to anger, not wanting any one to perish.[17] The Bible is filled with examples of when the Father stayed his anger at people's disobedience.

The Father is loving.

We have seen examples of his love through the care he took in the plan of Creation and the systems of law and justice he has established. But his love

---

16. Comfort, *Tynedale Dictionary*, 1275
17. Num 14:18; Ps 86:15; 103:8; 145:8; Exod 34:6, Joel 2:13; Jon 4:2; Neh 9:17

for us is also passionate and emotional. He loves us deeply and personally; not wanting *any one* to perish (2 Pet 3:9).

The Father is constant and never changing.

The Old Testament records thousands of years, showing the character of God, how he has been at work, and how he continues to be at work. Scripture also shows how God the Father has not changed, when he says, "I the Lord do not change."[18]

The Father is still in control of his great plan. He still loves his creations. He still works for the benefit of those who love him. Because the Father never changes, the basis for our trust in him remains constant. All aspects of the Father's character are good and never change. The reasons we have to trust him do not change. The New Testament also shows the unchanging nature of Jesus, divine God. Hebrews 13:8 tells us, "Jesus Christ is the same yesterday and today and forever."

We can trust the Father because he does what he says he will do

A covenant is an agreement or contract between two parties where each party agrees to do or not do something. In our earthly lives, if a person does not do what he says he will do, we consider that person untrustworthy. Only a person who does what they say they will do, is worthy of our trust.

God the Father promised many things to people in the Old Testament and then fulfilled every one of those promises. God does what he says he will do. Sometimes from our perspective, those things are bad. But from God's perspective, everything he does is for our benefit.

God's trustworthiness was evident at the beginning, when he promised, in a warning, that if Adam and Eve ate from the Tree of Knowledge of Good and Evil, they would die. They did eat the fruit. They were then restricted from eating from the Tree of Life. Thus, they died a physical death. God did what he promised. (We will see how that is actually a good thing for us.)

Later, God told Moses that if Moses would lead the Jewish people out of slavery, they would inherit the Promised Land—a place of prosperity.

---

18. Mal 3:6; see also; Ps 102:27; Jer 31:3

Moses led the people out of Egypt and God personally guided the millions of Israelites with his presence in fire and cloud. God did what he promised and loved his people by giving them his holy presence while completing that promise.

God told King David that David would have an heir on his throne to reign forever. King Jesus, David's earthly descendant, established his eternal kingdom. God did what he promised.

God said he loved mankind. He provided evidence of that love by creating everything for our enjoyment and by sending Jesus to provide his promised way for us to be with him eternally. God did what he promised.

Need more examples?

- God promised Abraham and Sarah that they would have a child, even though both were very old. Sarah gave birth to Isaac.
- God promised that Zechariah and Elizabeth would have a child in their old age. Elizabeth gave birth to John the Baptist.
- Shadrach, Meshach, and Abednego believed in all of the promises of God, giving them confidence to disobey the king and be thrown into the fiery furnace. They survived.
- God promised mankind that the one who will fulfill his promises will be born of a woman, be an Israelite, and a descendent of David. In the same context, God promised David that David's throne would be established forever. King Jesus, born through David's lineage fulfilled both promises—to mankind and to David personally.

The Apostle Paul tells us that God's promises will be fulfilled. God is not man. He is a divine being who guarantees his promises. We can therefore trust the Lord.[19] Joshua summarized it just before he led the Israelites across the Jordan River and into the Promised Land.

> "You know with all your heart and soul that not one of all the good promises the LORD your God gave you has failed. Every promise has been fulfilled; not one has failed."[20]

Scripture records songs and prayers of praise to God.[21] Those people praised God for what he had done in their lives and in the lives of the people

---

19. See 2 Cor 1:20; Titus 1:2; 1 Thess 5:24
20. Josh 23:14; 21:45
21. 1 Sam 2:1–10; Luke 1:46–55, 67–79; and many of King David's psalms

he loved, reminding them that God does what he says he will do. He keeps his covenants and promises. He cares for his children. He wants us to have a loving relationship with him. He waits patiently for us to choose him. We can trust God the Father because he does what he says he will do.

> **Connection Point**: God sometimes makes general but intensely powerful promises to the people who love him. Have you ever felt that God had made a personal promise to you? Has he fulfilled that promise? Are you still waiting for him to?

We can trust the Father because his plan is based on love

In human relationships, sometimes people may want us to obey them for reasons other than love, such as asserting power, manipulation, or other self-interest. God, however, already has infinite power. God already has or can create anything he wants. He does not need to manipulate people. Nor does God wield power over us for evil purposes. God does not want us to trust him to make himself feel good. Everything the Father does is out of love for us and for our good.

> And we know that in all things God works for the good of those who love him, who have been called according to his purpose (Rom 8:28).

In fact, we can trust the Father because of his love for us for several reasons:

First, we don't have to earn God's love. Sometimes we fearfully distrust someone who openly says he loves us without wanting anything in return. There must be something they're not telling us; something they'll get out of it, we think. But God loved us even before he created us—planning us with care and making sure the universe was prepared in advance for us. He then gave us stewardship over all of the world, trusting us with his creations, even before asking us to trust him. That is evidence that his motives are pure. He loves us simply because he does; not because of what we do or do not do.

> **Connection Point**: A mother loves her newborn infant simply because she does, not based on anything that infant did or did not do or ever will do. She has planned for her child's needs with

care, making sure her baby's nursery, clothing, and nutrition have been prepared in advance.

Second, God chose us first. Part of God's plan is for us to love him. But before we ever hear about him; before we ever experience his love; before we ever consider his plan for mankind, he loved us enough to choose us to be in his plan. He could have chosen the goats or the koala bears. After all, he loves them, too. But instead, he chose us people.

> **Connection Point**: Parents of a child whose birth was planned, chose to create that child. The parents of that child loved the child even before he was born. Those parents chose for that child to be part of their plan and their family.

Third, God wants us to know him. God's handiwork in the world can be seen by those who look for it. God's beauty can be found in nature. God's intelligence is evident in our science. God's working in people's lives is recorded in Scripture. God is there for us to find. He wants us to seek him and to know him. By knowing him, we will better understand the depth of his love for us.

> **Connection Point**: An infant does not instantly know his parents. But through the parents' care and nurturing, the child soon recognizes his parents. Gradually, an infant learns about his parents and understands the depth of their love for him.

Fourth, God wants us to love him in return. God does not want us to know him simply to be worshipped. He wants us to know him because when we do, our reaction will be to love him. It is the returned love he desires from us, knowing that when we know him, we will also love and worship him because his character is worthy of worship. He knows that loving and worshipping him will give *us* joy.

> **Connection Point**: After several weeks, an infant learns to smile. That smile is usually bestowed first on a parent. It is a simple way for the infant to react to the parent's love for him—a way to return their love.

Fifth, more than simply loving him, God wants a relationship with us. Part of that love relationship includes wanting that relationship to never end. The Father doesn't just desire that we love him temporarily in our earthly lives. God the Father wants a love relationship with us that will last forever.

Connection Point: A parent isn't just a parent for 18 years or until the child leaves home. A parent is a parent for his life and the life of his child. No parent ever wants their loving relationship with their child to end. They want a love relationship to last forever.

As Christians, the Holy Spirit lives in us. We can therefore now experience God in this world. But God the Father, still and always in Heaven, wants us to be in a relationship with him eternally where he is. The only way we can do so is to be made acceptable by the forgiveness provided through Jesus' blood sacrifice. In order for us to have an eternal, personal relationship with God the Father, as he desires—in this life through the Holy Spirit and eternally with him in Heaven—we must accept Jesus' gift of sacrifice. (Don't fret. We will look at why God needed a sacrifice in the next chapter.)

> This is good, and pleases God our Savior, who wants all people to be saved and to come to a knowledge of the truth (1 Tim 2:3–4).

One of the clinchers about why we should trust the Father and his plan, is that he does not force himself on us. God is not a bully. He offers us grace and mercy freely. He gives us evidence of his goodness and the goodness of his plan. Then he allows us to make a choice. Whether we choose to accept God's plan or not, is up to us.

Connection Point: Which of these reasons behind God's love for you impacts you the most? Which have you never considered? Which help you trust God more?

Remember that question people ask. "How can God say he loves us but then sends people to Hell?" God does not send anyone to Hell. Rather, God made a way for us to escape going to Hell. Then he made it even better. When we choose not going to Hell, we have also chosen to spend eternity in Heaven with him. In reality, it is we who send ourselves either to Hell or to Heaven. It is our choice, based on that free will God gave us to decide. That is our compassionate, loving God—giving us a way off the Highway to Hell and onto the Stairway to Heaven.[22]

22. See Appendix E about getting into Heaven if you have never heard about Jesus

We can trust the Father because his plan is good and he has given us the ability to choose either good or evil.

Chapter Summary

- **Theology Simplified:** God can be trusted. Examples of people in Scripture who trusted God with big things in their lives can give us a nudge toward beginning to trust God in our lives. We can also look at the Father's character and understand that it is worthy of our trust. Additionally, we can trust that God's plan is offered with no strings attached, because it is based on his love for us, from the very beginning, as the best thing we can have for our own lives.

- **What's it to me?** You may feel as if your faith isn't strong enough if you don't trust God in every aspect of your life. It is natural to withhold your trust of God, because it is based on your personal experiences with people. Even harder is trusting in something unseen. But God has shared examples of people who trusted him. He has given us evidence of his love and goodness. Personal experience can help us begin to trust God, to build on that trust, and to trust him more.

- **Faith Simplified:** God and his plan are trustworthy.

This is the first Principle in *Faith Simplified*: We can trust God and his plan.

Principle 2

Why Do We Need a Savior Anyway?

4

We Need Saving

The first sin

Back in the Garden of Eden, Adam and Eve lived in God's presence. God spoke with Adam, giving Adam instructions not to eat the fruit from the Tree of Knowledge of Good and Evil. After Adam and Eve ate that forbidden fruit, God walked through the Garden, personally looking for Adam and Eve. God was a real part of their lives on earth.

Then God sent Adam and Eve from the Garden because they disobeyed him. Now they no longer had access to the Tree of Life. They were therefore no longer immortal. They also no longer lived in relationship with God in his physical presence. By dying a mortal death, however, God implemented the method for Adam and Eve and all of us to return to God eternally, to live with him in Heaven after death—free forever from evil and in relationship with him forever. We'll look at death in more detail later as to how God made something good for all of humanity back then through death—something we generally consider horrible.

The first blood sacrifice

Let's dip our toes into that blood sacrifice question. When Adam and Eve disobeyed God, they recognized their nakedness. They had been running around the Garden all this time naked, thinking nothing of it. But when they sinned, they felt shame for disobeying God. That shame expressed itself partly in shame for their physical bodies.

Principle 2 | Why Do We Need a Savior Anyway?

So Adam and Eve took leaves and covered their nakedness. Did they think they could wear camouflage so God wouldn't find them? Maybe if they could postpone God finding them for long enough, he would have forgotten about their disobedience. Ultimately, God found them and he hadn't forgotten.

God knew that covering themselves with plants did nothing to cover Adam and Eve's sin of disobedience, yet he understood how their shame over their nakedness reflected the shame they felt about their sin. God therefore sacrificed his own creature for Adam and Eve and used the skin to cover their physical bodies. He showed his love in a concrete, practical way they could understand, by providing them with clothing that comforted them despite their shame.

> The LORD God made garments of skin for Adam and his wife and clothed them (Gen 3:21).

That sacrifice was also a representation of God covering their sin against him. God provided for himself the sacrifice he needed to pay for Adam and Eve's sin against him. Knowing God had killed one of his precious animals and had given the skins of that animal to Adam and Eve to wear, made the point better than what they tried to do themselves. Sewing a few plants together would never adequately cover their nakedness. Those skin garments however would have been a constant reminder, not only of God's love for them. The skin garments would also have been a constant reminder of their disobedience and the consequences of it—a death.

> **To illustrate the point:** Adam and Eve hide in the Garden just after eating the forbidden fruit. Eve gasps. God has just killed her lamb Snuggles right before their eyes. "No!" Eve cries. Adam had often laughed when the lamb came running to her as she called him by name.
>
> Now Snuggles lay in a pool of blood.
>
> "Why did you do that, God?" asks Adam. "Didn't you love Snuggles?"
>
> "Yes," replies God. "I love all of my creations. But you disobeyed me. Snuggles had to die so I could provide you with clothing to cover your nakedness. Snuggles had to die instead of you because the payment for disobedience to me is death. Snuggles made that payment for you."

It isn't enough, thinks Eve, that Snuggles lay dead on the ground. It isn't enough that she now wore Snuggles' skin. She and Adam were the ones who had disobeyed God, not Snuggles.

But Snuggles would never again nudge her to pet him. Snuggles would never again eat a bundle of grass from her hand. Snuggles would never again come running when she called.

God's voice softens. "Death is the price of sin," he says.

That first blood sacrifice instituted the sacrificial system that continued until Jesus. The sacrificed animals made Adam and Eve right with God once more—at least until they sinned again. But look closely at that sacrifice. Right at the beginning of humanity, God himself provided the blood sacrifice through one of his own animals. He sacrificed his own creature to himself that was needed to pay for Adam and Eve's sin. That was a clear foretelling of his plan for what Jesus would do later. Jesus—God in the flesh—provided his own blood sacrifice to himself to forgive our sins against himself.

What is Original Sin and why should I care?

We hear the term *Original Sin* bandied about in Christian circles. The term *Original Sin* is not found in Scripture. It is a theological concept that refers back to Adam and Eve. When Adam and Eve ate the forbidden fruit and disobeyed God, that was the very first, the original sin committed by mankind. Although Adam and Eve had personal consequences from their disobedience, and although God "covered" their sin with a blood sacrifice, that Original Sin lingers with humanity forever as a reminder that we are prone to disobedience.

Even though Adam and Eve had disobeyed God, He still loved them. In fact, in addition to providing the blood sacrifice to cover their sin, another major blessing came out of Adam and Eve's sin. God had made the world perfect and good. But when Satan entered God's perfect and good world, evil entered the world, too. The blessing consequence of Adam and Eve's disobedience is that by eating the fruit from the Tree of Knowledge of Good and Evil, they knew what good and evil was, right there after their first encounter with evil.

That gift—the knowledge of good and evil—remains with us today. Think of it as part of our spiritual DNA, giving us an inborn understanding of what is good and what is evil. It is one more example of how God took something bad that Adam and Eve had done and turned it into something for their (and our) benefit. What we do with the knowledge of good and evil is up to us. It's a gift with a responsibility.

In effect, the knowledge of good and evil because of that first Original Sin, is now a mechanism through which we can view the world, our actions, and the actions of others. It can help us choose how to live our lives. It is also a tool to help us process whether or not to pursue a relationship with God the Father, made possible by choosing to accept salvation through Jesus' blood sacrifice.

Scripture tells us that God makes each of us accountable for our own sins.[1] We are not to be punished for the sins of our ancestors. However, all of us have been marked by Adam and Eve's first, Original Sin. The consequences of that sin—banishment from the Garden, end of humanity's immortality (death), broken relationship with God, and knowledge of good and evil—remain with us.

> **Connection Point**: Have you ever considered the consequences of Adam and Eve's disobedience on your personal life? You do not now live in the paradise of Eden. You are a mortal being, who will die. You also have innate knowledge of what is good and what is evil, yet you often make decisions that result in disobedience to what God wants for your life. You cannot physically walk through the Garden with God. What might your life have been like if there had never been that first sin?

Original Sin does not refer to our personal, individual sins. But Original Sin remains with our souls, like an asterisk, reminding us that we are affected by the presence of evil in the world. Our free will, as evidenced by Adam and Eve's first bad choice of disobedience, has the power to cause us to sin.

Our individual sins

We are constantly facing choices we make as individuals. We live in a world surrounded by evil and temptations. The Apostle Paul reminded us of this fact when he said:

---

1. Deut 24:16; Ezek 18:19–20

We Need Saving

> For I do not do the good I want to do, but the evil I do not want to do—this I keep on doing (Rom 7:19).

No matter how hard we try, we sometimes make poor decisions. We do things we don't want to do or don't intend to do. We think badly about people. We want things that aren't ours. Though as Christians we are to battle with the world spiritually, we are nonetheless tempted by it and sometimes that temptation results in sin. That sin may be "insignificant" to the rest of the world. But if it is contrary to God's desire for our lives, it is sin. James reminded us of this, saying:

> If anyone, then, knows the good they ought to do and doesn't do it, it is sin for them (Jas 4:17).

Thus, part of our spiritual struggle with sin is that we need forgiveness.

The sacrificial system

As mankind grew in numbers, God chose to work through the Hebrew people in accomplishing his plan of salvation. That is what Scripture means when it says the Hebrew people became known as God's "chosen people." They were not inherently better, wiser, or less sinful than any other group of people. But their society did generally believe in God, despite falling away from him again and again. Although the sacrificial system had been around since Adam and Eve, it was through the Hebrews, that God codified it into law. The books of Leviticus and Numbers are filled with rules about who was to perform sacrifices, what constituted an adequate sacrifice, when and where the sacrifices were to be made, how they were to be performed, and what sins they covered.

Animal sacrifices, in the ancient Jewish sacrificial system, however, did not provide total forgiveness of sin. They only covered the sins, like whitewash. They covered the sins, in the same way God's sacrifice of his animal covered Adam and Eve's shame. Sacrifices did nothing to take away the stain from a person's soul. Nor did they cause God to completely forgive a sin. Not even a person's own blood could do that because a sacrifice required innocent blood. By definition, a sinner's blood is not innocent. Since animals were innocent though, they could die in place of the sinner.

But animal sacrifices were only a temporary fix. Sacrificing one lamb—even one lamb per person—was insufficient to cover all the sins humans committed. Sacrifices had to be done for each new sin and each new sinner. But why did God need a blood sacrifice at all?

Why blood?

To answer this question, we need to jump about Scripture between the Old and New Testaments. There, we learn that blood is the payment God requires.

> without the shedding of blood, there is no forgiveness (Heb 9:22).

God does not specifically tell us the reason for this, but Scripture clearly shows that blood was required to be shed, from the very beginning when Adam and Eve sinned. Leviticus hints at God's reasoning by saying that life is in the blood.

> For the life of a creature is in the blood, and I have given it to you to make atonement for yourselves on the altar; *it is the blood that makes atonement for one's life* (Lev 17:11; emphasis added).

For Greater Depth

We hear the word *atonement* here and there in Scripture when dealing with blood sacrifice. The specific Hebrew word for *atonement* used in Leviticus and related to sacrifice, is *kapar*. Interestingly, that word is the same Hebrew word used in Genesis for the tar Noah used to cover the ark. In other words, blood sacrifices were performed to cover (atone for; not forgive) the sins of people.[2]

The Jewish Day of Atonement—in Hebrew called Yom Kippur (shortened from *yom kippuriyam*) is still observed by modern Jewish people. *Kippuriyam* is a noun that means the act of reconciliation. During ancient Yom Kippur observances, animals were sacrificed on behalf of the community. Individual males could also pay ransom money (*koper*), to help them reconcile with God individually. From that practice, we get the reference

2. Zodhiates, *Dictionary*, 521.

in Scripture that Jesus' blood paid our ransom.[3] The ancient Jewish *koper* given by men on the Day of Atonement, was not required by God's laws. It was a tradition the Jewish people sometimes practiced to help them reconcile themselves to God. But that ransom was in addition to the blood sacrifice God required to cover their sins.

When it came to atonement, the Jewish sacrificial system required a payment to God to cover sin. Blood was the payment God required ever since the very first sin committed by Adam and Eve.

Scripture also says "the wages of sin is death" (Rom 6:23). When we are employed, we are paid wages, usually in money. The consequence of work is being paid money. When we sin, however, we are paid with death. Death is the consequence we get when we sin. Death is the currency when dealing with sin. In the ancient sacrificial system, the death involved an animal. That animal's death (and thus its blood) paid God for the covering of our sin.

Let's follow the scriptural reasoning. The payment used for atonement covering of sin is blood. Forgiveness of sin brings eternal life (Heb 9:22) and life is in the blood (Lev 17:11). It is all connected and set out clearly in Scripture. There had to be a sacrifice involving blood; there had to be a death to restore our right standing with God. Right standing with God (righteousness) results in eternal life.

We may not know why God required blood sacrifice, but we do know he determined that death is what paid for sin and that the death involved blood because blood is evidence (indication; sign) of life. Rather than dying themselves when they sinned, God allowed the Israelites to kill an animal. That animal's death paid to cover the sin. God required a blood sacrifice for sin from the very beginning.

> The blood of goats and bulls and the ashes of a heifer sprinkled on those who are ceremonially unclean sanctify them so that they are outwardly clean (Heb 9:13; the remainder of this verse to be discussed in the next chapter).

The Jewish people believed that one day a Messiah would become their Savior. They were taught meanwhile, that blood covered sin, like whitewash, which made them appear outwardly clean, and therefore right with God—at least as right as they could be by doing things on their own.

---

3. See Matt 20:28; 1 Tim 2:5–6

Principle 2 | Why Do We Need a Savior Anyway?

Connection Point: It is hard for us modern people to understand the importance that blood sacrifice was to the Jewish people, but God required those sacrifices since the beginning of the world. The Jewish people tried to be obedient to God's rules, so they continued to offer blood sacrifices to cover their sins and appear acceptable to God. Do you think you would look at sin differently (even "little" sins, such as disobeying a traffic rule now and then or using God's name as a swear word) if you had to personally take an animal to a priest to be killed as an offering to cover that sin?

The sacrificial system was complicated

In addition to having to continually offer blood sacrifices to cover each sin for each person each time they committed one, the Jewish sacrificial system included other aspects that made it complicated. Once the sacrificial system was codified in the book of Leviticus, sacrifices could only be performed by priests. Since only men from the tribe of Levi could be priests, only the Levites were able to perform sacrifices. Thus, if a person wanted a sacrifice performed, he had to ask a Levitical priest to perform it.[4]

Additionally, only certain animals could be sacrificed. Regulations clearly specified which animals were considered clean (acceptable to God) and which animals were not. Laws further specified how many of each type of animal were needed and what sins their blood covered.

Furthermore, sacrifices could only be performed at the Tabernacle (and at the Temple after King Solomon built it in Jerusalem). Before Moses wrote down God's instructions, people could offer sacrifices anywhere God considered holy, or any place God did not object to. For example, Noah offered sacrifices when he and his family left the ark; Abraham went to the top of a hill.

The Temple in Jerusalem was completely destroyed in AD 70 and was never rebuilt. Because sacrifices were required to be performed at the Temple, no further Jewish sacrifices have been allowed by the Jewish religion since then. If no Temple existed, sacrifices could not be performed. That remains part of the Jewish religion today.

---

4. Num 18:6–7

We Need Saving

To illustrate the point: Let's look at how the Jewish sacrificial system might work in our modern world if traffic laws were God's laws.

You are driving down the freeway. The car in front of you moves into the right lane but doesn't signal. "Sacrifice one goat," the giant electric Sacrifice Sign flashes in enormous bold letters. The car edges off the freeway to a roadside sacrificial booth.

"Ha!" You yell through your window. "You should have used your turn signal, buddy!"

A red sports car zips past you, 20 miles over the speed limit. "Sacrifice a goat and a lamb," the giant electric Sacrifice Sign flashes in enormous bold letters. The car edges off the freeway to another roadside sacrificial booth.

"Ha!" You yell through your window. "You shouldn't have been speeding, buddy!"

A car pulls up behind you, honking and veering back and forth—way too close to your car. "Sacrifice a lamb," the giant electric Sacrifice Sign flashes in enormous bold letters. The car edges off the freeway to another roadside sacrificial booth.

"Ha!" You yell through your window. "You need to learn how to drive, buddy!"

Your phone rings. It's your boss so you pick up the phone and answer it. "Sacrifice a goat, a lamb, and two pigeons" the giant electric Sacrifice Sign flashes in enormous bold letters.

You groan, muttering, "talking on the phone while driving." You hang up on your boss, slamming the phone down harder than necessary, and edge off the freeway to the next roadside sacrificial booth. There, carcasses of animals lay in a pile. The smell of decaying flesh makes your nose twitch. You inch your car through a puddle of blood, waiting your turn in line. You hand your credit card to the officer to pay for the goat, the lamb, and the two pigeons your disobedience has cost. A flurry of black flies zip into your car. You swat at them in annoyance.

The officer swipes your card and nods you forward. In your rear view mirror you see a goat, a lamb, and two pigeons being wrestled forward by a man wearing a red splattered apron. An enormous knife is sheathed over his shoulder, like an ancient warrior.

PRINCIPLE 2 | WHY DO WE NEED A SAVIOR ANYWAY?

Your stomach tightens. Poor creatures. But at least they will die to cover my disobedience to the law, you think. I'll definitely remember never to talk on the phone while driving again. Even if it is my boss calling.

You head up the entrance ramp to return to the freeway, a smile on your face, now that your driving problem is taken care of. You safely merge into traffic. "Sacrifice one goat," the giant electric Sacrifice Sign flashes in enormous bold letters.

"Rats!" You edge off the freeway to the next roadside sacrificial booth. "Turn signal. Gets me every time."

The Jewish sacrificial system was complex. It regulated what animal, for what sin, by whom, and where sacrifices were to be performed. All of these regulations, along with the fact that sacrifices were required at all, meant that for the Israelites, their faith was a system of works. Obey the laws and when you don't, sacrifice animals to cover your sins with blood. It was about getting right with God by what you did. And what you had to do back then was complicated. It was also temporary.

The sacrificial system only provided temporary coverage

Under the Jewish sacrificial system, what mattered most was obedience to God's law. Obedience equaled righteousness in their eyes. If you sinned, obedience to the law meant that you were required to offer a sacrifice. The sin was covered. Done deal. But not eternally a done deal.

We saw that the sacrificial system was about "covering" sin with blood. This covering appeased God, making the person right with him temporarily. Think of it as covering the sin by "clothing a person in temporary righteousness"—just as the first sacrifice clothed Adam and Eve's physical bodies. The stain of the sin on a person's soul however, remained. Thus offering an animal's blood sacrifice did not obtain God's complete forgiveness. Rather, blood sacrifice made you right with or acceptable to God, for now. You were right with God about that one sin; until you sinned again.

Earlier we discussed Yom Kippur, the Jewish Day of Atonement. It is an example of this temporary nature of sacrifice. Each year, on the Jewish Day of Atonement, five animals were brought to the Temple—including two goats. One of the goats was sacrificed. The priests then spiritually or symbolically placed the sins of the people onto the second goat and sent it out into the wilderness. That goat was the *scape goat*, who carried the sins of the people with it, away from the community. That goat was not sacrificed; those sins were carried away symbolically; but not forgiven. And symbolically, that goat still carried their sins around with him as he roamed the wilderness. This ceremony had to be repeated every year, because there were always new sins.

The Jewish sacrificial system wasn't true forgiveness. Rather, it was a continual process. "You are right with God until . . . the next sin." Because there was always a next sin, a person could never be completely right with God forever.

The Jewish people strove to be obedient. God had told them what to do. He had codified the rules and the sacrificial system for them. They did the only thing they could do—work hard to be obedient. Their belief in salvation was "faith by works" and it was not enough. They could be "right with God" temporarily, but they could never be completely forgiven by what they themselves did, or by what a priest did on their behalf.

Then Jesus came and completed the sacrificial system once, for all people. No longer did people have to do something to be right with God. No longer did people have to try to earn their own salvation. Jesus simplified the entire process. We have nothing to do. We only have to accept Jesus' offer, confirming our belief that he did it all.

Chapter Summary

- **Theology Simplified:** God required blood sacrifice to deal with our sins. The original sacrificial system was complicated and cumbersome, but it was the only system God had provided to make us right with him.

- **What's it to me?** One of the obvious benefits of Jesus' sacrifice is you don't have to kill all those animals. A priest no longer has to sprinkle blood on you. In fact no longer does anyone have to do anything. One more thing to be grateful for when it comes to salvation through Jesus.

- **Faith Simplified:** God requires blood to cover sin. Because we sin, God established a system for sacrifices. Now all that is required to be right with God is to believe in Jesus.

5

How Did Jesus Change Things?

We can't earn salvation

THE ONLY WAY THE ancient Jewish people could be right with God was by working hard to follow God's rules and be obedient to him in all ways. When they weren't obedient, it was a sin. They then had to offer blood sacrifices to cover those sins so they were outwardly acceptable to him. Faith was about people doing things on their own to make themselves righteous (right with God).

Nonetheless, that right standing was temporary. The people were considered righteous as long as they followed the rules; their sins were covered until the next time. And underneath it all, their souls retained Adam and Eve's spiritual asterisk of Original Sin indicating mankind's tendency to sin. And sin, humanity did. And does. And will do.

Other religions require a person to try to work his way into Heaven or nirvana or become enlightened by what he does. Even Judaism, which is the root faith in God upon which Christianity is based, required people to attain salvation by doing things on their own.

To illustrate the point:

- In Hinduism, salvation can be achieved by doing good works, by individual study, and by acts of devotion, through cycles of birth, death, and rebirth. It is based on what you do.
- In Buddhism, salvation is achieved by personal discipline and meditation. It is based on what you do.

- Salvation in Islam is accomplished by worshipping Allah, repenting of sins, and hoping Allah will forgive you. It has a focus on doing good works. Blood sacrifice is still a part of Islam, done during a person's required pilgrimage to Mecca. Salvation is based on what you do.

Christianity, on the other hand, is the only faith that is based solely on what someone else—Jesus—did. Jesus provided the sacrifice. Jesus made us acceptable to enter Heaven. There is nothing we humans can do to make ourselves acceptable or righteous enough or perfect enough to enter perfect Heaven on our own. The one and only requirement in order to get into Heaven, is believe that Jesus is who he says he is; that Jesus did it all for us. When we make that single decision—choose to believe in him—boom! We are saved. We do nothing to get into Heaven, because Jesus already did everything needed.

Salvation through Jesus was always part of God's plan

From the beginning, the Father's big plan included his plan for our salvation through Jesus. Wait a minute, you say. Jesus didn't even show up until the New Testament times. Ah, but he did. Scripture tells us that Jesus is the one who spoke all things into existence.

> In the beginning was the Word [Jesus], and the Word was with God, and the Word was God. He was with God in the beginning. Through him all things were made; without him nothing was made that has been made (John 1:1–3; explanation added).

For Greater Depth

> Jesus existed from the beginning. That part of Christian theology is called *preincarnate Jesus*. *Pre* means before. *Incarnate* means in the flesh. In other words, *preincarnate Jesus* refers to Jesus' existence before his physical human birth in Bethlehem.
>
> John tells us that Jesus existed in the beginning and spoke the world into existence. Jesus tells us that no one but him has seen the Father. Certainly God's Spirit doesn't walk or talk audibly. When Jesus showed up in the Old Testament, however, people recognized him as God. They didn't know him by his earthly

Principle 2 | Why Do We Need a Savior Anyway?

> name of Jesus. They simply called him "Lord" or "the Lord." Those appearances of Jesus before his birth are called *theophanies* or *Christophanies* in Christian theology.

It is clear from Scripture that Jesus existed in the beginning. Then a few thousand years later . . .

> The Word [Jesus] became flesh and made his dwelling among us. We have seen his glory, the glory of the one and only Son, who came from the Father, full of grace and truth (John 1:14; explanation added).

Jesus was fully a part of the Father's plan from the beginning. Jesus revealed his part of God's plan frequently during his ministry. He told us that the reason he lived was to pay for our sins.

> "the Son of Man [Jesus, referring to himself] did not come to be served, but to serve, and to give his life as a ransom for many" (Matt 20:28; explanation added).

We saw earlier that blood was the *ransom* to pay for sin ever since Adam and Eve's first sin. It was a temporary *Get Out of Jail Free* card for the Jewish people. In Jesus' time on earth, blood sacrifice was still the way God dealt with sin. Rather than continue the system of sacrificing animals forever, Jesus paid the ransom for everyone's sins with his one death. Jesus, God himself, completed the plan of salvation. Jesus offered everyone a *Get Out of Jail Free Forever* card—no fine, no punishment, not even a punitive court appearance in front of the Judge.

Just like he did for that first Original Sin, once again, God provided his own blood sacrifice to cover mankind's sins. But this time, the blood sacrifice he provided was himself, in the person of Jesus. And this time the sacrifice was sufficient not just to cover sin but to forgive it. We'll look at that sufficiency later in this chapter.

But you ask: Did God change his plan after Adam and Eve sinned? Surely God's plan for us was to always live in the Garden of Eden and never die, right? Evidently, it was not.

Death was always part of God's plan

We read the account of Adam and Eve's fall from grace and moan, wishing they hadn't eaten the forbidden fruit. If they hadn't, we'd all still be lounging in the Garden, never dying, noshing on fruit, hanging out with God, never worrying about what we should wear. But when Adam and Eve disobeyed God, God's justice required them to have a consequence for their poor decision. The physical death part of God's plan began.

When sin entered the world, Holy God no longer walked amid it. Thus, when God sent Adam and Eve from the Garden, mankind could no longer enjoy a one-on-one relationship on earth with him. That one-on-one relationship with God was broken. Death for mankind, however, was not a change of plans. It wasn't a quick fix. It wasn't God's do-over. We know death was always part of God's plan for mankind, because of what Scripture says.

Before Adam and Eve ever disobeyed God, before they ate the forbidden fruit, God told Adam,

> And the LORD God commanded the man, "You are free to eat from any tree in the garden; but you must not eat from the tree of the knowledge of good and evil, for when you eat from it *you will certainly die*" (Gen 2:17–18; emphasis added).

"You will certainly die," God said in his instructions. Death was not a concept God later thought up after Adam and Eve sinned. Physical death was something God had in mind for his creations—well before they disobeyed and ate the forbidden fruit.

Why would God's good plan for us include death? That certainly doesn't sound "good."

But it was. If we never died, our souls would be trapped in our physical bodies forever. We can't take a plane to Heaven. We can't walk there. We can't physically travel to Heaven at all. But by dying, our eternal souls are set free from the physical world. Choosing salvation through Jesus, is the way our souls can eventually live in relationship with God, safe from evil, in Heaven forever—if we are first made sinless. It looks like this:

> Earthly life followed by
> mortal death followed by
> spiritual eternity somewhere
> either in Heaven or Hell.

Principle 2 | Why Do We Need a Savior Anyway?

Scripture reveals that God designed and implemented the system of death at the beginning of humanity's life on earth. Our part is to choose where our soul will spend eternity; where it will go when it is released from our physical body.

> **Connection Point**: As Christians, we know that death is what begins our eternal life with God. Yet we cling to this life. It is counter-intuitive, to think of death as something good. Death feels more like a punishment mankind is given because of what Adam and Eve did. Does the idea of freeing your soul from the physical world give you a hint that death might not be a horrible thing?

Jesus' salvation returns us to a relationship with the Father

Jesus' blood sacrifice provided salvation for us, making us acceptable to the Father, if we choose him. Death then provided a way for us to eventually return to a relationship with God. Death does this in two ways.

First, through our death: if we have accepted Jesus' gift of his sacrifice, we are forgiven. The blotches on our soul caused by sin disappear. When we die a physical death, having been forgiven, we are acceptable to live in sinless Heaven—forever in God the Father's presence. Death enables us to be in an eternal one-on-one relationship with God the Father.

Second, through Jesus' death: When Jesus returned to Heaven, he left us the gift of the Holy Spirit. The Holy Spirit—God's Spirit—lives in each person who believes in their salvation through Jesus. We believers therefore are able to live with the presence of the Holy Spirit and in communion with him—as a promise of eternal life with the Father to come. We are able to live in a one-on-one relationship with God, the Holy Spirit, while we are still physically living here on earth.

In other words, the Father's plan is so filled with love and compassion, that he used even death to enable us to live in his presence, now and forever.

Why Jesus?

Most often the animal sacrificed in ancient times was a lamb. That is the significance behind what John the Baptist said when he saw Jesus.

> "Look, the Lamb of God [God's own sacrifice] who takes away [not just covers] the sin of the world" [everyone]!" (John 1:29; explanation added)

Jesus provided God (himself) with his own blood sacrifice of himself. We no longer have a need for animal sacrifices that merely "cover" sins.

> The blood of goats and bulls and the ashes of a heifer sprinkled on those who are ceremonially unclean sanctify them so that they are outwardly clean. How much more, then, will the blood of Christ, who through the eternal Spirit offered himself unblemished to God, cleanse our consciences from acts that lead to death, so that we may serve the living God! (Heb 9:13-14)

Now our sins can be completely forgiven and the stain on our souls gone—if we accept Jesus' sacrifice. But, you wonder, why could it only be Jesus' blood? Why could Jesus be the only appropriate sacrifice?

Jesus was sinless

> And in him is no sin.[1]

While animal blood is innocent and was used to deal with sin before Jesus' earthly ministry, we saw that it only covered sin temporarily. Jesus, being God in the flesh, was also sinless. In fact, when asked why only Jesus could be the blood sacrifice, Christians usually respond, "Because Jesus was sinless." Yes, he was. However, he is not the only one.

> **To illustrate the point:** Imagine a brand new infant. That infant has never sinned. It is innocent. It is sinless. Why didn't God just sacrifice a sinless baby?
>
> What a horrifying idea! Of course, God wouldn't require us to sacrifice a baby to deal with our sin. In fact, more than a dozen Old Testament verses specifically record God's hatred of people who sacrifice their children.[2] That's a whole lot of verses revealing God's feeling about child sacrifice.

---

1. 1 John 3:5; see also Heb 4:15; 2 Cor 5:21; 1 Pet 2:22
2. Deut 12:31; Lev 20:1-5; 2 Kgs 3:27; 23:10; 17:17-18; Ps 106:37-38; Jer 7:31; 32:35; Ezek 16:20-21; 20:32; 2 Chr 33:6; and Gen 22 God's rejection of Abraham's sacrifice of his son, Isaac

Even sacrificing an innocent infant wouldn't be enough to forgive our sins though. The proper sacrifice for our eternal salvation had to be more than just sinless.

Jesus was worthy

Jesus is worth way more than a lamb or a goat or even a sinless human if one could be found. Jesus' sacrifice didn't cover just one sin for one person. Jesus, God's sacrifice of himself, was of such worth that it could cover all sin for all people for all time—all people who ever lived and who would ever live. That's worthy!

Then, because of Jesus' worth, God went a step further—to address not just a *covering of sin* but complete *forgiveness*. Here's the tough theology broken down:

Only God can forgive sin.
Only God is sinless.
Only God is worthy of himself.
Only a sacrifice *of* God can provide the sacrifice worthy of God's own forgiveness of sins against himself.

If mankind sacrificed every animal who ever lived, it wouldn't be enough. No matter how much God loves his creations—including those precious lambs and goats—their blood sacrifice isn't worth enough in his eyes to cover or forgive the sins we have committed against him. Sins against God are that big; that overwhelmingly important; that damaging to our relationship with him. Only a sacrifice of God himself to himself is worthy enough to forgive sins committed against him. We couldn't provide an adequate sacrifice ourselves, so God provided it. Of himself. To himself. For us.

Jesus was infinite

God never runs out of himself. Therefore, only sinless Jesus, as God, sacrificing his infinite (boundless, limitless, inexhaustible) self, one time on the cross, provided an innocent (sinless), adequate (infinitely worthy), and forever sacrifice to not only cover sin, but to forgive all sins for all people who ever lived and who would ever live.

Let's look at the King James Version of Matthew 26:28.

For this is my blood of the new testament, which is shed for many for the remission [forgiveness] of sins (explanation added).

Most of us are more familiar with other versions of this verse which translate what Jesus said, that Jesus' sacrifice was for the *forgiveness* of sins. The King James Version quoted above, uses the word *remission*. What does that mean?

For Greater Depth

> The original Greek word used in Matthew 26:28, translated as *remission*, is *aphesis*. In addition to forgiveness, the definition adds the releasing a person's guilt over his sins. It includes an element of delivering the sinner from the power (but not the presence) of sin by radically changing that person's desire to avoid sin in the first place. It is these aspects of the definition of *remission of sins* that Christians refer to freedom from the slavery of sin.[3]

The old sacrificial system was straightforward: blood sacrifice covered sins. Because Jesus, as God, was worthy and infinite in nature, in addition to sinless, his own blood sacrifice was sufficient to forgive all (each and every) sin of all people who have ever lived and who would ever live. In fact, not only did his sacrifice forgive sin, it had the power to deliver the sinner from the control of sin over us. Jesus did not do away with the sacrificial system. He completed it. We no longer have to sacrifice animals. In fact we do not have to do anything. We only have to choose to believe that Jesus did it all for us and accept that gift.

We each have the right, duty, and power to decide whether or not to accept Jesus' gift of forgiveness. We cannot save any other person by making that decision for them. Only Jesus can save a person. In fact Jesus already has, if each person accepts that salvation for themselves.

Jesus took it four steps further

First: In addition to providing a blood sacrifice that is more than adequate to forgive each and every person's sins for all time, Jesus' blood sacrifice

---

3. Zodhiates, *Dictionary*, 295–296

forgave sin backwards in time to Adam and Eve. Every sin ever committed could be forgiven because it was God who was sacrificing himself. He had the power and authority to deem his own sacrifice sufficient and acceptable for all people, for all time, including the people who would live after Jesus' earthly death. That includes us! And every person born after us.

Jesus' sacrifice is deemed sufficient also for people who died before him, if they died in faith. God knew whether or not those people loved him. God knew whether or not they looked forward in faith to a way they would be made eternally right with him. That faith in God and his plan essentially constituted a "yes" to Jesus' future offer of salvation. They were forgiven and now spend eternity with him (Heb 11:13–16).

Second: Jesus made a way for us to be in relationship with God. Originally, mankind (Adam and Eve) lived in the Garden in the presence of God. God walked with them physically and spoke to them. When they sinned, they were cast out of the Garden. Their relationship with God was broken. They (we) then became sinful beings who could not be allowed eternal life in perfect, sinless Heaven, because with us there, Heaven would no longer be perfect and sinless. Fortunately forgiveness deletes sins from our soul. We become sin-less. Forgiven, sin-less people are therefore allowed eternal life with the Father in Heaven.

Third: We are promised that we can also live our earthly lives here with God. When we accept Jesus' gift, he awakens in us our recognition of the Holy Spirit. The Holy Spirit—one third of the Trinity—is God living not just with us but in us—guiding, directing, counseling, and befriending us. We receive the gift of living with God, not only in the future forever, but right now in this life also. You'll see how important the Holy Spirit is to our salvation later in this book.

Fourth: Once we have received Jesus' gift of forgiveness and the gift of the Holy Spirit, we are freed forever from the requirement of performing endless blood sacrifices. To return our love for what Jesus has done, the Apostle Paul reminds us, then that we are to be a living sacrifice.

> Therefore, I urge you, brothers and sisters, in view of God's mercy, to offer your bodies as a living sacrifice, holy and pleasing to God—this is your true and proper worship (Rom 12:1).

This living sacrifice points us back to Leviticus 17:14. Life is in the blood. But now, the blood is not the blood of a sacrificed animal who died. Now the blood is ours—as living beings. We don't shed our blood in sacrifice. Rather, we live a life of sacrifice. Our lives, because of our life-giving blood, are meant to be lived in a way that honors and glorifies God because of what Jesus did.

Chapter Summary

- **Theology Simplified:** Jesus completed the system of blood sacrifice not just to cover sin but to forgive sin for all people for all time. Forgiven people are seen as sin-less through God's sinless eyes. That makes us eternally acceptable and allows us to be with the Father in Heaven. But first we must accept Jesus' sacrifice to forgive our sin and make us sin-less.

- **What's it to me?** Many Christians live with shame over decisions they made before they said "yes" to Jesus. Jesus—God himself, the one who spoke the whole, great big, wonderful universe into existence—provided the perfect, adequate, suitable, acceptable sacrifice that was powerful and worthy enough to forgive whatever sin we committed or will ever commit. Whatever sin. As his forgiven child, he has chosen to look at you through his sinless eyes and see you as sinless, too. If God does that, perhaps you can begin to see yourself the same way.

- **Faith Simplified:** Jesus became the blood sacrifice to end the complex sacrificial system and forgive everyone; as part of the Father's plan. To be forgiven and live eternally with the Father, we only have to choose to do so.

This is the second of five principles of *Faith Simplified* which this book is based on: We need a Savior.

Principle 3

Why Did God Make So Many Rules and Do I Have to Follow Them?

6

Commandments One Through Three

When God first created man and woman, he gave them only one rule: Don't eat from the Tree of Knowledge of Good and Evil. One rule? How hard could it be to follow just one rule? Really hard, evidently.

As with many things, God took something bad and made something good from it. Although eating that forbidden fruit was a sin, it gave Adam and Eve and thus all of us, the ability to discern good from evil, at the very time sin and evil entered our world. The ability to recognize good from evil, combined with God's gift of free will to decide whether to pursue good or evil, should have been enough to keep us on the right path of choosing good at all times.

It wasn't.

God's rules are to benefit us

Mankind spent the next millennia without any new clarified rules from God. The world without rules, however, ultimately became a mess. It got so bad, in fact, that except for eight people and a boatload of animals, God destroyed all life and started over.

It wasn't long after Noah, that the world was a mess again. By Moses' time, mankind had grown in numbers and society had become more complex. In the Father's timeline, Jesus' arrival on earth was not scheduled for another two thousand years. Until then, mankind desperately needed guidance. So, God codified for his chosen people—the Israelites—ten rules for living.

God did not give us the Ten Commandments because he needed us to behave. He did not give us those rules for his own advantage. God did not give us those rules for our salvation. He gave us those rules so we might have better lives here and now, in this earthly life.

> **Connection Point**: Have you ever stopped to think that your life is better when you follow the Ten Commandments? Would the world be better if we all followed them?

As we look in detail at each of God's ten rules for better living, we need to remember an important point. Although God's plan is detailed and intricate, whenever the plan is something for us to do, God keeps it simple. It is usually we who complicate things; or forget that God lovingly does things for our benefit. Additionally, understanding the essence of God's codified laws, makes what Jesus did even more astounding and wonderful.

The first three commandments deal with our relationship with God. So let's look at them and how they are for our benefit.

Commandments One and Two

> You shall have no other gods before me (Deut 5: 7).
>
> You shall not make for yourself an image in the form of anything in Heaven above or on the earth beneath or in the waters below. You shall not bow down to them or worship them (Deut 5: 8–9).

We can look at both of these two commandments together because they go together. At first reading, it sounds like they are for God's benefit—as if he selfishly wants our worship. But that doesn't make sense. God is anything but selfish.

Why Commandments One and Two are important

God made humans with an inherent fascination about him. We may look for God in nature or science. Others may stubbornly try to convince themselves (and others) that he does not exist at all. The truth is that humans spend a lot of their time and effort on the issue of God—whether seeking God, proving his existence, or trying to disprove it. Throughout the history of mankind, most every recorded society has worshipped a deity of some

Commandments One Through Three

form, even if it was just a carved piece of wood. With that in mind, and without thinking too deeply, we recognize that life is a lot easier with only one God to worship. No worrying about seven or eight deities, each with a different set of rules, holy days, customs, and traditions. But the value to us of Commandments One and Two is deeper than life being easier.

Second, God knows that only he is worthy of our worship and nothing else is. Images crafted by human hands have no power. They are merely pieces of wood or rock or metal. Nor can a tree or a star help us in life. God knows we are wasting our time, effort, and lives if we worship anything other than him.

Worship does not just refer to the 20 minutes we sing praise songs at church. Worship may take the form of singing. Or it may take the form of prayer, giving, doing, being, serving, or any other activity we engage in to honor God for the holy being he is. Whatever form it takes, worship is our response to God. But the value to us of Commandments One and Two is deeper than devoting our worship to something other than God.

Third, Scripture tells us that God is a jealous god (Exod 20:5). From human perspective, jealousy never ends well. If a jealous person seeks revenge, that jealousy makes many people miserable. This commandment, however, does not refer to God's revenge if we worship something other than him.

For Greater Depth

> The original Greek word used to describe God as jealous is *quanna*.[1] The definition includes an aspect of zeal—great energy and enthusiasm to protect and benefit his people. Joel 2:18 tells us that the Lord was *jealous* for his land and took pity on his people, providing them with corn, wine, and oil and sending the enemy's army into a barren, desolate land. Similarly Zechariah chapter 8, tells us that God's jealousy meant he would dwell in Jerusalem, the city would be filled with men and women living to a "ripe old age," and boys and girls would play in the streets. God's jealousy in those instances was a wonderful thing for his people.

---

1. Zodhiates, *Dictionary*, 1000–1001

God knows that the further we pull away from him, the less joy we have in our lives. God cares about relationships—his with us, ours with him, and ours with each other. Worshipping God brings us closer to him. Being closer to God results in joy. Having a better relationship with God blesses us.

God's jealousy is *for* us; *over* us; *on our behalf.* He loves us enough to jealously guard us so we are not led away from him toward something of no value. God's jealousy is a loving example of his desire for our good. God is not jealous of a piece of rock carved in the shape of a cow—or the time and importance we place on career, wealth, or accumulation of things. Rather, God is jealous for the wasted effort we might expend in such a focus. God wants that time and effort directed toward him because he knows that when we direct ourselves toward him, we are blessed.

Both of these first two commandments emphasize our recognition of who God is. God wants us to understand our relationship with him as the ruler of all things. He wants us to understand our personal status within that relationship. We are not God's equal. We are not his pal. God is not just the big guy upstairs. God is above us in all things and we are to worship and serve only him. Despite our unequal status with the King of the Universe, God allows and encourages us to approach his throne of grace. He gives us free will to choose him.

God wants a relationship with us. But the relationship is to be that of our Heavenly Father and his beloved child. These two commandments help us recognize the proper relationship we should have with him.

> **Connection Point**: Are you a parent? If so, after you had a child, did you better understand what your relationship with our Heavenly Father should be?

What did Jesus have to say about Commandments One and Two?

> "Away from me, Satan! For it is written: 'Worship the Lord your God, and serve him only'" (Matt 4:10).

Jesus also said:

> "No one can serve two masters. Either you will hate the one and love the other, or you will be devoted to the one and despise the other. You cannot serve both God and money" (Luke 16:13).

In both of these verses, Jesus pointed out the importance of focusing on, worshipping, and serving God, rather than anything else. We can remember that God is worthy and worshipping him brings us into deeper relationship with him. That is definitely for our good.

Worship is to recognize the difference between you and God and show reverence for him. Serving him is about knowing who God is in order to commit yourself to him.

Connection Point: Have you taken that step in committing to worship and serve him? If not, keep reading. (If so, keep reading anyway.)

Commandment Three

> You shall not misuse the name of the LORD your God, for the LORD will not hold anyone guiltless who misuses his name (Deut 5: 11).

Commandments One and Two specify that God should be the priority in our lives. Understanding our place in a relationship with him will bring more peace in our lives. Commandment Three involves how we honor God. Commandment Three tells us we are to uphold the holy character of God by not misusing his name.

What does it mean to misuse God's name?

Most of us think this commandment simply tells us not to use God's name as a swear word or an expletive. While that is true, there is more to it.

First, we are not to make oaths to God we do not intend to fulfill. Oaths are covenants. Throughout history, God has worked through covenants. In Scripture, God promised to do something if people only . . . did not sin . . . worshipped him . . . believed. God still works through covenants. Marriage, for example, is a covenant between two people and God; he being the higher authority in that relationship.

The biblical definition of *testament* is covenant (agreement). The entire New Testament section of our Holy Bible therefore is God's new covenant (new testament; new agreement) with us. It is his oath, in effect. He promises salvation through Jesus, because of what Jesus did. God the Father's part of the covenant is that he will forgive us and grant us eternal life with him if we choose to believe that Jesus is our Savior (our part of the covenant).[2]

Connection Point: Let's pause to let that sink in. God has a covenant with you personally. He has guaranteed to forgive you for absolutely anything you might have done, no matter what, if you believe in Jesus and ask for that forgiveness. Can you think of something you have done that you have not yet asked forgiveness for? Now is a great time to ask.

For Greater Depth

> Some versions of Scripture translate Commandment Three as not taking the Lord's name in vain. The original Hebrew word used in this specific verse is *saw*. The biblical definition of *vain* here is: useless, worthless, without result. It includes in its general meaning emptiness, vanity, evil, ruin, deception, fraud, deceit, falsehood.[3]

Notice that the biblical definition of the word *vain* above, includes deception, fraud, deceit, falsehood. In the context of oaths in God's name, taking his name in vain would mean making an oath you did not intend to keep. It would be lying, attempting to deceive or defraud while basing the oath on your relationship with God. When we make an oath in life, we are to base that oath on our belief in God. Modern court proceedings, for example, used to require us take an oath to be truthful, by placing our hand on the Bible. Doing so in effect, is promising to tell the truth based on who God is and who we are in relation to him.

The damage to us personally when we make an oath in vain is to our integrity. Our reputation, honesty, and honor, once damaged, are difficult to repair. We spend our lives building integrity, being honorable, doing what is right. We are held in esteem by others. We represent Christ in how we live. Thus, not taking God's name in vain when making an oath, protects other people's rights and well-being. It also protects our personal integrity and helps us exemplify Christ to others.

2. Zodhiates, *Dictionary*, 424–428
3. Baker, *Dictionary*, 1107

Commandments One Through Three

Misusing God's name also has to do with the power God's name holds.

> No one is like you, Lord; you are great, and your name is mighty in power (Jer 10:6).

Again and again, Scripture tells us to pray with power, using God's holy name. There is power in God's name when we pray. It holds authority. On the other hand, when we misuse God's name by praying without recognizing the power his name holds, we diminish the power we believe God controls for our benefit. Put another way, it diminishes the faith we have in prayer because, in our minds, we give up some of God's power to work in our lives. Of course, God's power itself does not diminish. But we diminish our ability to accept his authority in our lives when we do not have faith in that power. More of God's power at work in our lives is clearly a benefit to us.

Prayers that do not include faith in God's power may still be granted if it is God's will to do so. But from our perspective, such prayers contain elements of being useless, worthless, without result—praying without recognizing God at work. We end our prayers *In Jesus' name*. We petition God the Father for what we need, what others need, what we desire. We do so in Jesus' name—Jesus, as God the Son. In that way, we are calling on the power Jesus' name holds. To not utilize and rely on the full power of God's name is to use it vainly—uselessly, worthlessly, without result.

Connection Point: When you pray, do you have faith in God's power to answer your prayer in the way that is best for you?

What did Jesus have to say about Commandment Three?

> "All you need to say is simply 'Yes' or 'No'; anything beyond this comes from the evil one" (Matt 5:37).

Jesus' comment has to do with making promises. A promise is an oath or a covenant. Here Jesus focused on maintaining our integrity. He told the people not to worry about making oaths, but to simply say "yes" or "no" and then do what you said you would do. He basically told us not to misuse God's name by making oaths to other people that you cannot or do not intend to keep, but simply be truthful in our relationships.

Jesus also taught us to pray in his name, as God's Son.

> "And I will do whatever you ask in my [Jesus'] name, so that the Father may be glorified in the Son. You may ask me for anything in my name, and I will do it" (John 14:13–14; explanation added).

Jesus took ownership of the power and authority given to him by the Father—passing access to that power to us when we pray in his name.

God's name reflects his holiness, authority, and power. He wants us to remember the holiness, authority, and power of his name. He wants us to not use his name in a manner that is irreverent or worthless. It reminds us of our place as children of the Most High God. Being children of the Most High God is a blessing, for sure.

Chapter Summary

- **Theology Simplified:** The first three commandments help define what our relationship with God should be, including our worship of him and remembering that even his name is holy.

- **What's it to me?** Why would anyone want to think of themselves as equal to God? We aren't. We can't be. We shouldn't bother trying. Instead, you can remember that *you are God's child*. And he loves you individually and passionately. That makes it easy to worship him.

- **Faith simplified:** God wants us to recognize our place in a relationship with him—as his loved children.

7

Commandment Four

COMMANDMENT FOUR COMES RIGHT after the first three commandments that show us how to have a right relationship with God.

> Observe the Sabbath day by keeping it holy, as the LORD your God has commanded you. Six days you shall labor and do all your work, but the seventh day is a sabbath to the LORD your God. On it you shall not do any work (Deut 5:12–14).

Our need for rest

While every day of the week is holy, Commandment Four shows that God knows we need rest. It is as if God is saying, "I love you enough to tell you to take a break from the daily grind." As a result of being refreshed and rested, we are able to then return to work and be more productive in what we accomplish.

Note that this commandment doesn't tell us we have to attend a church service on any particular day of the week—or even at all. Rather, we should work for six days and then rest on the seventh, using God's own example of Creation. There is more to a need for physical rest, however, in this commandment.

For Greater Depth

> One key to understanding this commandment are the definitions of *labor* and *work*. The two words in Commandment Four are not the same Hebrew word. The original Hebrew word for *labor* here is *abad*. This word means worship or service focused on other people or God. The word does not have connotations of toilsome labor or economic livelihood. Instead *abad* includes an experience of joyful liberation.[4]
>
> The Hebrew word used in Commandment Four for *work* however is different. *Work* in this specific verse is the Hebrew word *melakah*. This word means occupation, business, agricultural tasks, referring generally to the economic toil we do to provide for ourselves and our families.[5]

Wait. Are we supposed to rest from joyful experiences of focusing on God as well as from our toil? Heavens no! A careful look at this verse, says that we *abad* (worship God and serve him and others) for six days. We also work and toil (*melakah*) for six days. On the seventh day we are to rest from our *melakah*. It does not say, however that we are to rest from *abad*-ing. The joyful experience of focusing on God and serving others is to continue seven days a week. That seventh day, we can rest in God.

Resting in God

Hebrews expands on this idea of resting in God.

> There remains, then, a Sabbath-rest for the people of God; for anyone who enters God's rest also rests from their works, just as God did from his. Let us, therefore, make every effort to enter that rest, so that no one will perish by following their example of disobedience (Heb 4:9–11).

---

4. Baker, *Dictionary*, 795
5. Baker, *Dictionary*, 614

For Greater Depth

> Notice that the book of Hebrews talks about a sabbath-rest; not a sabbath day of rest or any specific 24-hour period. The Hebrew word sabbath does not mean Saturday or any particular day of the week. It does not even mean seven as in the seventh day of the week. Rather, sabbath comes from the Hebrew verb *sabat*, simply meaning to rest, to cease work.[6]

Resting in God means more than just resting from physical work. It means setting mental and emotional drudgery aside. It means pausing to leave your worries with God. It means being quiet to listen more closely to what God might be telling you or teaching you or leading you to appreciate. It means seeking to understand a bit more about God's character or his plan or his love. Resting in God means drawing close to him and being refreshed.

Come near to God and he will come near to you.[7]

When we rest from our toil (*melakah*), on whatever day that is, we are then better able to focus on our labor (*abad*)—our joyful experience worshipping God and serving him and others. When we worship God and help others, we stop thinking about ourselves and start acting more like Jesus.

Commandment Four sits right between the first three commandments about our relationship with God and the final six commandments about our relationship with others. Not coincidentally, when we have rested—physically, emotionally, and have drawn closer to God so that we are spiritually rested—we are then able to have more patience, compassion, and grace with people in our lives. This commandment is clearly for our benefit.

Put into perspective, we are to *abad* all seven days of the week. It does not matter which of those seven days we might choose to attend a community worship service, or at all. It does not matter because every day we worship God brings us joy. The point is to take one day in seven to rest from toil so as to worship God and serve him and others more fully every day.

6. *King James Dictionary*, s.v. "sabbath (n.)"

7. Jas 4:8; see also Heb 4:16; 7:25; 10:22; Ps 73:28; 145:18 about the blessings of drawing near to God

Connection Point: God intends us to spend one day each week to remember who he is—the creator, the all-powerful, all merciful being who wants you in his family. Every week you do not take time to remember who God is, is a week you drift further from him. How might you take time each week to *abad*—serve others and focus on God? Do you think you would have more peace and joy in your life if you did?

What did Jesus have to say about Commandment Four?

Periodically, Jesus went off by himself. Did he spend the day dozing or skipping rocks? No. Scripture tells us he spent time with his Heavenly Father, gaining strength, guidance, and encouragement for the next days of his ministry. Jesus modeled how we should live, including taking time to focus on God.

> "The Sabbath was made for man, not man for the Sabbath. So the Son of Man is Lord even of the Sabbath."[8]

Jesus also said,

> "Come to me, all you who are weary and burdened, and I will give you rest" (Matt 11:28).

Jesus reminds us that he gave us this commandment of sabbath rest for our benefit when he said, "The Sabbath was made for man." Jesus, as God, created Commandment Four in the first place and therefore exercises authority over his own rules and regulations, including sabbath rest. That understanding is key to recognizing Jesus' justification for performing miracles on the Jewish Sabbath day.

Matthew 11:28 further reminds us that Jesus came to provide us with rest from having to work to achieve our own salvation. Before Jesus, people believed they earned righteousness through works—specifically by trying to obey God's laws. Now, however, when we come to Jesus, Jesus gives us rest from that work because his sacrifice resulted in God the Father's grace and mercy. We no longer have to work to earn God's favor. We have rest from working to try to gain our own salvation.

---

8. Mark 2: 27–23; see also Matt 12:8; Luke 6:5

Chapter Summary

- **Theology Simplified:** God knows we need rest from our daily work; but not from worshipping and serving him and others. Spending time with God deepens our relationship with him. Jesus' grace means we do not need to work to earn our salvation or God's favor. We can rest in what Jesus did for us.

- **What's it to me?** One day in seven God wants you to rest in him; focus on him; feel his love for you. This commandment is another practical example of how he has expressed his love in a concrete way. Resting in God can give you both the physical and spiritual rest you need to equip you for the days ahead. It is a blessing. Enjoy it as the gift he intended.

- **Faith Simplified:** Spending time with God fortifies our relationship with him and gives us strength and joy for life. We need that each and every day of our lives. We need to rest in him.

8

The Final Six Commandments

Getting Along with Others (Even the Annoying Ones)

THE FIRST THREE COMMANDMENTS have to do with our relationship with God. Commandment Four deals with our relationship with God as well as how that relationship improves our relationships with people in our lives. The final six commandments relate to our relationship with others. Our pursuit of those commandments though are all affected by our relationship with God. And following those final six commandments improve our lives.

Commandment Five

> Honor your father and your mother, as the LORD your God has commanded you, so that you may live long and that it may go well with you in the land the LORD your God is giving you (Deut 5:16).

Most children have good parents. Those good parents deserve the respect of their children. Therefore, this commandment at first seems easy for many of us to follow. Underneath its simplicity, however, is the tougher issue of how to honor bad parents and how to forgive them.

What about bad parents?

This commandment does not say we must honor the actions, inactions or ungodly character traits of earthly fathers or mothers who were bad parents. Rather in particular instances, we may have to simply honor the position of father or mother, as you would honor the Office of the President even if you disagree with a particular president's politics.

The beauty of this commandment further is that if we cannot honor the actions or character of our own father or mother, we can release judgement of them to God, knowing he sees their hearts and will deal with their judgment eternally. That releasing of judgment is part of the forgiveness process. Forgiveness is not about declaring an action or a person OK, when clearly that action or character trait is wrong or harmful. It is also not about us ignoring the need to protect ourselves or others from harmful action by that person in the future.

Rather, forgiveness is about letting the matter go emotionally. It is about recognizing consequences that have happened because of that person's action but releasing eternal judgement to God to take care of. Our forgiveness of others is about making the free will choice to leave it up to God so that the other person's spiritual judgment is no longer our responsibility (and never was).

That sometimes feels impossible to do. We've been hurt. We are resentful. Our trust with other people is affected. God recognizes all of that and never tells us to "give them another chance" or "forget everything they ever did." Rather, forgiving others is recognizing that God will give those people their eternal "comeuppance" (what they deserve). It is recognizing and trusting that whatever comeuppance God decides to give them is just. It is trusting in God's character—not theirs.

Inheritance

The second aspect of Commandment Five has to do with inheritance. God gave the Jewish people this commandment at the time in Jewish history when he was leading them into the Promised Land. The land they would enter would be divided among the twelve tribes of Israel. Family honor thus not only had to do with family unity; it also had to do with property ownership. If family honor was maintained between parents and children, children were likely to inherit that property and live long in the (promised) land the LORD gave them.

While inheritance in our modern world is of less relevance, when we look at Commandment Five, the value to us is still to encourage family unity and to encourage parents to be honorable in raising their children so as to earn honor and respect from them in return.

Raising children

This commandment is also about a parent's duty to teach children about God. Just after the Ten Commandments set out in Deuteronomy, are additional instructions to parents.

> Impress them [the laws] on your children. Talk about them when you sit at home and when you walk along the road, when you lie down and when you get up (Deut 6:7, explanation added).

Proverbs summarized the duty of a parent, saying

> Start children off on the way they should go, and even when they are old they will not turn from it (Pro 22:6).

In other words, a good parent teaches his children about God, discussing spiritual matters as part of everyday life. A child of such a good parent will naturally honor the parent for doing so because the child has learned to look at life in a way that honors God. One of the tragedies in the Old Testament, as well as in modern times, is that when parents fail to teach their children about God, the children fall away from God and society suffers.

When parents have honorably taught their children about God, his teachings are passed from generation to generation. The result is that people live long (or at least have blessed lives) in the land here on earth God has given them.

This commandment begins the final six commandments about our relationship with others by focusing on the people we were in relationship first—our parents. It is also perfectly placed to remind us to honor our Heavenly Father. When we honor him, living a life of faith, our (eternal) lives will be long in the heavenly land where he will allow us to reside.

What did Jesus have to say about Commandment Five?

> "Anyone who loves their father or mother more than me is not worthy of me; anyone who loves their son or daughter more than me is not worthy of me" (Matt 10:37).

Jesus also said,

> "Who is my mother, and who are my brothers?" Pointing to his disciples, he [Jesus] said, "Here are my mother and my brothers. For whoever does the will of my Father in heaven is my brother and sister and mother" (Matt 12:48–50, explanation added).

The point of these two verses is not technically about honoring our parents. Matthew 10 is about a kind of love different from love of family. Jesus is telling us that love of God is a higher, deeper kind of love in action. Matthew 12 furthers the idea of love for family, saying all who do the Father's will are part of Jesus' eternal, heavenly family.

Jesus often referred to the Ten Commandments. He never disputed the value of Commandment Five. Rather, he used well-understood family relationships as a way to teach about our relationship with our Heavenly Father and what our relationship with Jesus should be. Our love of God and our desire to do his will should take priority over even our relationship with our earthly family.

God wants us to honor the first people who were part of our lives. An improved relationship with people in the closest relationship to us is logical. Forgiveness of bad parents and releasing judgment of them to God unburdens us.

> **Connection Point**: What is your relationship with your parents? Your children? Are your parents worthy of honor or do you need to leave justice to God? Are you worthy of your children's honor?

Commandments Six, Seven, Eight, and Nine relate back to Adam and Eve. When they disobeyed God, they became able to know right from wrong. Before that, there was no choice about good and evil for Adam and Eve to make. In the Garden, everything was good. Once in a world filled with good and evil, they then had to make free will choices about whether to embrace good or evil.

Because we modern people have that innate knowledge of good and evil passed down from Adam and Eve, instinctively, we know that murder, adultery, stealing, and purposely damaging someone's character are wrong. Those commandments therefore are God's reminders to us of what we already know is wrong. By writing down the things we should know anyway, God gave us a baseline to refer to. Satan is skilled at using truth as well as lies to subvert God's desires. By having them written down, it is harder for Satan to get us to ignore them.

Additionally, while we might instinctively know good from evil, having laws set out by God specifies that doing evil is a sin against God. Just recognizing evil isn't enough. God wants us to not sin by participating in evil. Paul points that out to us, saying

> I would not have known what sin was had it not been for the law (Rom 7:7).

So, what are the final five commandments? Why are they for our benefit?

Commandment Six

You shall not murder (Deut 5:17).

Notice this commandment does not say you shall not *kill* others. If that were the case, people in the military would be in trouble with God by their very career choice. Nor does it say it is a sin to accidently kill someone. We know God does not consider accidently killing someone a sin, because he specifically told the Israelites to set up cities of refuge where people who had accidently killed a person could go to escape retribution by the person's family, pending trial.[1]

For Greater Depth

> Some Bible versions do translate this word as *kill*. The original Hebrew word used in this verse, however, is *rasah*. The definition of *rasah* is not just *kill*. It specifically includes murder as part of its definition. While murder involves killing, killing does not always involve murder. A clearer translation of *rasah* for this verse is therefore murder, not kill.[a]

---

1. See Exod 21:13; Num 35:6–29; Josh 20
2. Baker, *Dictionary*, 1074

Our emotions

This commandment is about how we deal with other people based on emotions. Murder involves a blackened heart towards another person. The sin of hatred may have already been committed. This commandment recognizes that carrying out those feelings through murder is in addition to the feelings themselves. This commandment deals with acting based on emotion, addressing the sequence of events that lead to murder:

- Emotion: hatred, greed, jealousy
- The mind: what do I want to do with that emotion? Develop a plan
- The heart: Commitment to follow the plan
- Action: do the deed; commit murder

God of course wants us to be free from malevolent feelings toward others in the first place. He provides us with his forgiveness as the first step in cleansing our hearts and encouraging us to forgive others in the same way. But, while he is working to change our desires, we are to not do certain things we may want to do.

Following this commandment encourages us to not act on a murderous state of our emotions, which would result in consequences of societal judgment, imprisonment, and possible capital punishment for the crime of murder. This commandment is meant to keep us as productive, participatory members of society and to protect us and our loved ones from such action by others. Following this commandment is for our benefit.

> **Connection Point**: Have you ever been mad at someone and stewed for days before finally bursting out and telling them how angry you are? Did they respond with confusion, not understanding why you are angry? Or were they just as angry as you? How different would things have been if you had worked out the problem at the time it occurred?

What did Jesus have to say about Commandment Six?

> "You have heard that it was said to the people long ago, 'You shall not murder, and anyone who murders will be subject to judgment.' But I tell you that anyone who is angry with a brother or sister

PRINCIPLE 3 | WHY DID GOD MAKE SO MANY RULES

> will be subject to judgment. Again, anyone who says to a brother or sister, 'Raca [worthless; empty; empty-headed, indicating utter contempt] is answerable to the court. And anyone who says, 'You fool!' [wicked; morally worthless, scorn concerning a person's heart and character] will be in danger of the fire of hell.
>
> "Therefore, if you are offering your gift at the altar and there remember that your brother or sister has something against you, leave your gift there in front of the altar. First go and be reconciled to them; then come and offer your gift."[3]

Jesus restates Commandment Six and adds a challenge to it. Not only is it critical to avoid the action of murder, we also need to address the emotions behind murder. In fact, all emotions that divide human relationships are bad.

The importance of this commandment is to focus on relationships with others. Jesus is telling us not to let anger or ill will grow. In fact, says Jesus, God doesn't even want to see a gift from you until your heart is clear of anger in your relationships. Be reconciled with others and then approach God.

In short, Jesus reminded us that murder is a sin. Then he addressed what leads to murder: emotions.

Commandment Seven

> You shall not commit adultery (Deut 5:18).

Adultery defined

In both the Old and New Testaments, the meaning of adultery was sex between a man and a married or betrothed woman. Whose family you belonged to in Moses' time was important. Property ownership was granted to the various clans of the Israelites when they entered the Promised Land. After that, property was passed down within a family and kept within the particular clan it had been originally given to. It was therefore especially important to maintain family lines. Adultery caused problems of inheritance for the man's children, because a child resulting from adultery meant

---

3. Matt 5:21–24; added explanations in brackets are from Zodhiates, *Dictionary*, 504 and 1001–1002

the possibility of property going outside the man's own clan to the child of a woman from a different clan.

The modern definition of adultery has been expanded to simply mean sex between a married person and someone not his or her spouse.

Adultery begins with acting on our own desire. Adultery then brings another person into a sinful situation with us. Murdering someone is a sin one person generally commits on his own. Adultery involves two people sinning. Adultery then takes the consequences a step further. Adultery is not only a sin involving oneself and one's adulterous partner. It is also a sin against one's spouse, against the spouse of the adulterous partner, children of the people involved, and against God.

Remember the marriage covenant we looked at in chapter 6? When we marry, we promise to be faithful. In a Christian ceremony, that promise is made to our spouse. It is also made to God. Those promises are a covenant. When we break that covenant, we break a promise to our spouse. We also break a promise to God. In effect, when we break our marriage covenant, we have not only broken Commandment Seven, we have also broken Commandment Three. We have broken the oath we made to God in the marriage covenant. We have misused his name.

When people commit adultery, it becomes a barrier standing in the way of a healed, more wholesome marriage. God wants his children to honor their commitments to each other as well as to him. Avoiding the pain of broken marriage relationships by obeying this commandment is for our benefit.

Like for Commandment Six, this commandment addresses the sequence of events that leads to adultery:

- Emotion: lust
- The mind: what do I want to do with that emotion? Develop a plan
- The heart: Commitment to follow the plan
- Action: do the deed; commit adultery

What did Jesus have to say about Commandment Seven?

> "You have heard that it was said, 'You shall not commit adultery.' But I tell you that anyone who looks at a woman lustfully has already committed adultery with her in his heart" (Matt 5:27–28).

Jesus focused on people's hearts. The Old Covenant God made with his people was about obedience and following rules. Jesus taught to change people's hearts so they would never get to the point of sinful disobedience. In Matthew 5, Jesus explains that adultery begins with emotions. Emotions are where the issue needs to be addressed.

In the verses following Matthew 5:27–28, Jesus tells us it is better to gouge out your eye or cut off your hand if it causes you to sin. Scholars universally agree that Jesus wasn't implying we should poke our eye out preemptively. Rather, Jesus was using exaggeration to express how important it is to stop the emotions before they result in loss of self-control and sinful behavior.

This commandment is for our benefit. Although inheritance is no longer of primary importance in our society, stable marriages and families are a blessing. God wants us to have that blessing.

> **Connection Point**: Has your family or someone you know experienced pain resulting from adultery? How was each person hurt by the actions of two people? Do you think the people who committed adultery think the consequences were worth it?

Commandment Eight

> You shall not steal (Deut 5:19).

Stealing is taking what is not yours.

Outwardly, this commandment is about property ownership. Everything in this world, however, belongs to God in the first place. He entrusts us with his stuff. If we take something from someone who has been entrusted with God's stuff, we are not only stealing from that person, we are also stealing from God. If God wanted us to have it, he would have given it to us or shown us a way to obtain it. This commandment to not steal is to protect everyone's property ownership. The result of everyone's obedience is that ownership would be preserved. Relationships would be protected.

This commandment is also about contentment. Eve didn't learn the lesson to be happy with what God gave her. Rather, she wanted what she didn't have; the fruit God had not given her. This is a reminder about what

Eve had to learn. In the same way, this commandment relates to Commandment Ten: Do not covet.

This commandment addresses the sequence of events that leads to stealing:

- Emotion: greed, envy, jealousy
- The mind: what do I want to do with that emotion? Develop a plan
- The heart: Commitment to follow the plan
- Action: do the deed; steal

Like Commandments Six and Seven, this commandment also begins with emotions. The culmination of disobeying these last six commandments, is that we have failed to control those emotions. This commandment is a reminder to be content with what we have.

What did Jesus have to say about Commandment Eight?

> "You know the commandments: 'You shall not murder, you shall not commit adultery, you shall not steal, you shall not give false testimony, you shall not defraud, honor your father and mother.'"[4]

Jesus also said,

> "If you want to be perfect, go, sell your possessions and give to the poor, and you will have treasure in heaven. Then come, follow me" (Matt 19:21).

Commandment Eight has to do with our desire for stuff. Jesus quoted the commandments, reaffirming that they were good. The rich young man in this story told Jesus that he kept all of those commandments and asked how to obtain eternal life. Jesus responded, that to become *perfect*, he needed to sell his possessions and give to the poor.

For Greater Depth

> The Greek word for *perfect* used in this verse is *teleios*. As it relates to people, *teleios* means whole or complete. It is about becoming

---

4. Mark 10:19; see also Luke 18:18–30; Matt 19:16–30

> the person God intends us to be and reflecting God's holy perfection in our lives. In Matthew 19:21, *teleios* has the additional meaning of keeping yourself unspotted from the world.[5]

Effectively, Jesus told the man to keep himself from being tempted by things in the world, including wealth. Selling his possessions and giving to the poor would be a step in the process of becoming perfect (unspotted). It was the part of Jesus' response having to do with possessions which troubled the rich young man. Jesus knew that wanting things is a hurdle for many people. Commandment Eight recognizes our struggle and encourages us to be content with what God has given us. In fact, here Jesus further encourages us to give away even our desire for such things in order to obtain what is more valuable—eternal life.

Mark and Luke's version of this event, include Jesus' instruction for the man to then follow him. By following Jesus, the man would learn how to be whole and complete in his faith. By following Jesus, the man would understand that the only way to have eternal life was through Jesus.

> **Connection Point**: How do you deal with a desire for stuff? Are you able to let the desire go? Do you suffer because your desire is unmet? Would focusing on what you do have help you overcome this issue?

Commandment Nine

> You shall not give false testimony against your neighbor (Deut 5:20).

False testimony defined

Many verses of Scripture indicate God's general displeasure with lying. This commandment, however, is not strictly about lying. It has to do with treating others fairly. One of the greatest (or worst) things we own is our integrity. This commandment is about not causing injustice to someone

---

5. Zodhiates, *Dictionary*, 1372

else or damaging their reputation. If we testify against someone, knowing they will be found guilty or their reputation harmed, our testimony had better be the truth.

This commandment is also about our own esteem. It can be a human tendency to put other people down in order to raise our own status in other people's eyes. The reasoning is that if we hurt others' reputation, our own reputation might be seen as higher by comparison. God recognizes this inclination of ours.

God knows our actions. He knows our hearts and judges based on those. God wants us to witness honestly about others, because he himself is honest with us. Therefore we need to speak the truth. We especially need to speak the truth about our neighbors, both when in court as well as avoiding gossip. God wants us to live together in peace. Life is better when we live in harmony with others.

Like Commandments Six, Seven, and Eight, this commandment addresses the sequence of events that leads to false witness:

- Emotion: hatred, envy, jealousy
- The mind: what do I want to do with that emotion? Develop a plan
- The heart: Commitment to follow the plan
- Action: do the deed; witness falsely

What did Jesus have to say about Commandment Nine?

Jesus spent much of his ministry teaching about not trying to think of ourselves as better than others.

> "But the things that come out of a person's mouth come from the heart, and these defile them. For out of the heart come evil thoughts—murder, adultery, sexual immorality, theft, false testimony, slander" (Matt 15:18–19).

About our integrity and the integrity of others: Sitting down, Jesus called the Twelve and Jesus said, "Anyone who wants to be first must be the very last, and the servant of all" (Mark 9:35).

Jesus also said, "For all those who exalt themselves will be humbled, and those who humble themselves will be exalted" (Luke 14:11).[6]

---

6. See also Mark 10:45; Matt 20:28 about how we are to model how Jesus sees others

Matthew 15 reminds us that false testimony (and slander), along with murder, adultery, sexual immorality, and theft come from an evil heart. He also reminds us that our integrity is important. So is the integrity of other people.

Jesus loved everyone—even the people who hated him. He dealt with everyone as having value, including people who were otherwise shunned by society. Jesus' ministry sought to get rid of the old way of punitive judgment. No longer were we to deal with other people harshly or seek revenge. Jesus instead presented something radically new. He modeled God's grace toward us and taught that we were to apply the same grace toward other people in our lives.

The way we are to approach grace toward others is by looking at all people as having value. We are to recognize that we are no better than they are, nor do we have more value than they do—especially to God. Therefore we are not in a position to treat them judgmentally. When we approach our relationships with people in that way, we are humbled. That humility pleases God and exalts us in his eyes. Being exalted in God's eyes is way better than attempting to exalt ourselves in our own eyes or the eyes of others.

This commandment encourages us to be truthful, especially when someone else's integrity and legal rights are involved. It is intended to help maintain harmony in our relationships. A life filled with harmonious relationships is for our benefit.

> **Connection Point**: Have you experienced a time when someone put another person down clearly in order to try to raise their own esteem? Were you able to see through that attempt? How did it make you feel toward the person trying to raise his own esteem?

Commandment Ten

> You shall not covet your neighbor's wife. You shall not set your desire on your neighbor's house or land, his male or female servant, his ox or donkey, or anything that belongs to your neighbor (Deut 5:21).

What is contentment?

This commandment follows along with Commandments Seven and Eight about adultery and stealing. They are all about wanting what doesn't belong to you. This commandment then goes a step further. This commandment reminds us of the Apostle Paul who told us that he has learned to be happy in any circumstance—whether in need or in plenty.

> I have learned to be content whatever the circumstances (Phil 4:11).

Commandment Ten is about that contentment Paul refers to. A key word in Paul's comment is that he *learned* to be content. Contentment wasn't something he started out with. He worked at it. He learned contentment through struggle. More importantly, he learned contentment by relying on God for everything.

God has given us things in our lives. We should enjoy them. They are for our benefit. Our neighbor has been given things for his enjoyment, too. They are for his benefit. This commandment encourages us to be content with what we have and not focus on what others have.

Jesus told us that he came so that we may have life to the full (John 10:10). That does not mean we get every material thing we desire. It does not mean our every wish will be granted. Part of it does imply that, like Paul learned, when Jesus is at the center of our lives, our spiritual lives will be full, now and eternally.

Contentment is about focusing on what we do have; not on what we do not. It is looking at the glass of water and not simply seeing it as half full. It is also about realizing that the water in that glass is the living water of Jesus. It is about understanding everything living water entails—cleansing, forgiveness, satisfying our thirst for righteousness, and eternal life with Jesus forever. This commandment to be content with what we have now and what we will have forever, is for our benefit.

Commandments Six, Seven, Eight, and Nine all have to do with acting on human emotions to get something we want (covet). People hate someone else's life, so they murder to take that life. People desire someone sexually, so they commit adultery. People want someone else's things, so they steal. People are envious of others' reputation, so they falsely testify against them. All of those things have to do with emotions of wanting and then taking what doesn't belong to us. Commandment Ten sums it all up—don't act on your emotions. Be content with what you have.

What did Jesus have to say about Commandment Ten?

> "The thief comes only to steal and kill and destroy; I have come that they may have life, and have it to the full" (John 10:10; some Bible versions translate *to the full* as *abundantly*).

Jesus also said,

> "So do not worry, saying, 'What shall we eat?' or 'What shall we drink?' or 'What shall we wear?' For the pagans run after all these things, and your heavenly Father knows that you need them. But seek first his kingdom and his righteousness, and all these things will be given to you as well. Therefore do not worry about tomorrow, for tomorrow will worry about itself. Each day has enough trouble of its own" (Matt 6:31–34).

And Jesus said,

> "Blessed are those who hunger and thirst for righteousness, for they will be filled" (Matt 5:6).

It is God's desire for us to have a life filled with the good things he gives. The only thing we should hunger after and seek (desire, want, yearn for, covet) though is righteousness. Fortunately, there is no need to covet righteousness because Jesus gives that righteousness freely when we seek him. One of God's greatest gifts to us is that we can learn to trust him and receive contentment as a result of that trust.

> **Connection Point**: Have you learned to be content—with stuff, opportunities, your relationship with other people? How might focusing on your relationship with God help teach you about contentment?

Chapter Summary

- **Theology Simplified:** The last six commandments deal with our relationships with other people and with contentment. We gain contentment by following Commandments One through Three to establish a right relationship with God and following Commandment Four, to find rest in Jesus so we can better focus on our relationships with God and others.

- **What's it to me?** God wants you to have a good relationship with him now to prepare you for your eternal relationship with him in Heaven. He will not compromise on that. While you are living on this earth, however, you are also in relationship with people. Some of those people you like. Some you love. Some you try to avoid. God knows life is better here when we all get along. Life is also better when you are content with what he has given you.
- **Faith Simplified:** God gave us rules so we could get along with others. Basically, it is: do unto others as you would have them do unto you.

9

The 613 Were God's Laws, Too

GOD GAVE US THE Ten Commandments for our benefit—to live good lives and to encourage a deeper relationship with him. But what about the rest of those laws set out in Exodus, Leviticus, Numbers, and Deuteronomy? Weren't all those hundreds of laws just something Moses made up himself? Are they of any value once Jesus arrived on the scene? A large batch of our Bible preserves those laws. God recorded them for us for a reason. Let's see why.

Scripture tells us that after writing down the Ten Commandments, God then dictated additional laws to Moses (often called the Law or Laws of Moses). We can see they were given by God and not made up by Moses, because they are in quotation marks with God or the LORD tagged as speaker. For example, Exodus 21:1 begins the setting out of the laws, by God telling Moses, "These are the laws you are to set before them." Bible scholars debate over how to count the actual number of laws. For our purposes, we'll just refer to them as the 613 laws.[1]

To simplify things, let's divide the 613 laws into two categories:

Laws relating to God
Laws relating to the world

---

1. Scripture does not number the individual laws. The figure 613 is one of the most common calculations of laws noted by biblical scholars.

Laws Relating to God

The priesthood

Before God gave Moses the Ten Commandments, God specifically set apart the firstborn Jewish children as his own—to be used in his service. We see this specified "on the very day the LORD brought the Israelites out of Egypt."

> The LORD said to Moses, "Consecrate to me every firstborn male. The first offspring of every womb among the Israelites belongs to me, whether human or animal."[2]

For Greater Depth

> The Hebrew word for *consecrate* in this verse is *qadas*. *Qadas* means to sanctify, to dedicate, to show oneself as holy. To help further define *consecrate*, the word *sanctify* means set apart as holy. *Holy* means belonging to God and becoming holy as a result, because everything God owns is holy.[3]

In other words, before God set up the Levitical priesthood (the priests from the tribe of Levi), the firstborn human male of each family was consecrated (set aside) to the service of the Lord within that family to perform religious rites and ceremonies for that family. Although official priests existed before Moses' time, their specific role, duties, and selection process were not recorded in Scripture; perhaps never clarified at all.

In the desert, however, God appointed Aaron and Aaron's sons as priests who would perform the religious duties on behalf of the Israelites,[4] later adding the entire tribe of Levi to serve as priests. (For more about why God selected the Levites, see Appendix F.) The Levitical priesthood did away with disorganized priestly selection. Instead of every firstborn male being set apart in service to the Lord, now only the tribe of Levites would serve him.

---

2. Exod 13:1–2; 4:22–23; 22:29–30
3. Baker, *Dictionary*, 980
4. Num 3:10–14

"They [the Levites] are the Israelites who are to be given wholly to me. I have taken them as my own in place of the firstborn, the first male offspring from every Israelite woman."[5]

The Levitical priests became the spiritual intermediary (agent, mediator, facilitator) between God and the Israelites and served God on behalf of his people. Many of the 613 laws commanded by God therefore related to the function and service of the priesthood. It was something brand new for the Israelites.

The Tabernacle

The Tabernacle was the tent where God's presence resided during the Israelites' wandering before entering the Promised Land. The Tabernacle was dismantled, carried, and set up throughout the 40-year desert journey. Once the Israelites entered the Promised Land, the Tabernacle was set up in a permanent location in Shiloh. Several hundred years later, King Solomon built the stone Temple in Jerusalem to replace the Tabernacle tent structure.

Five chapters of the book of Exodus (Chapters 35–40) contain instructions and intricate specifications from God on how the Israelites should build the Tabernacle. The Tabernacle, after all, would hold the Ark of the Covenant which contained God's presence. The Ark of the Covenant would sit in a very specific place within the Tabernacle—called the Sanctuary or Holy of Holies or Most Holy Place. Only the one selected High Priest within the Levitical priesthood was allowed to enter the Sanctuary.

The sacrificial system

Many of the 613 laws provided for animal sacrifices to atone for (cover) sins. Various sins are spelled out in these laws. Types of animals that could be sacrificed were specified. When, where, how, and by whom sacrifices were to be performed was codified. Additional non-blood offerings were also defined. God proactively set up a system of sacrifices to cover each sin a person might commit. The book of Leviticus clearly portrays God's love for his people. For every sin a person might commit, God had a way to cover that sin or atone for it through sacrifice.

---

5. Num 8:16, 3:11–12; explanation added

Sacrifices were also performed over the millennia by pagans who sacrificed to their own gods. Those pagan sacrifices had become a perversion of what God intended. The land the Jews were entering was occupied by pagans. God's people therefore needed laws to make sure his sacrificial system was both understood and implemented correctly.

> **Connection Point**: A pagan was a person who believed in multiple gods. It also could refer to a person who did not believe in any god. How do you feel about calling people today who do not believe in God "pagans"? Does that sound strange?

Laws Relating to the World

Within the category of "the world" are laws on how the Israelites were to establish a government, have relationships with other nations, and how to establish a system of justice. Those laws dealt with business—including laws about agriculture, loans, treatment of employees, and good business practices. Other laws dealt with daily life, such as dietary laws for healthy living, family structure, sinful relationships, sexual rules, and general rules about relationships with others.

In essence, rules relating to the world have to do with how the Israelites' society would function and how the Jewish people would deal with each other in a large community and with the rest of the world. After centuries of slavery, the Israelites left Egypt as a loose group of approximately eight million men plus women and children. They then spent 40 years wandering the desert, led by Moses and administered by Aaron's priesthood. After 40 years without roots, God knew the Israelites needed guidelines for what came next.

> **To illustrate the point:** Let's look in on Joshua, standing before the Israelites as they get ready to enter the Promised Land.
>
> "After Moses died and I took on the leadership of this great family, I worried," said Joshua. "How could I lead our people safely? How could we establish a new nation when we have never done that before? How could we create a society of people who worked well and lived in harmony with others? How? How? How?"

Principle 3 | Why Did God Make So Many Rules

Joshua paused. He looked out over the people and held up the book of the law which God had dictated to Moses. "God not only provided for our past journey and our present place as we enter the Promised Land," Joshua said. "God also provided for our future, giving us rules to live by, to govern by, to worship him by."

The clouds moved away, allowing the morning sun to shine on the people.

"Now," said Joshua, "fear the Lord and serve him with all faithfulness. Choose for yourselves this day whom you will serve. As for me and my household, we will serve the Lord."

All the people shouted. "Praise God for his faithfulness!"

The hundreds of laws dealing with the world were to help the Israelites move from a nomadic existence to becoming a nation of millions of people who had never before functioned as a political entity. Looking at them that way, a couple hundred fairly simple laws to establish a society and rule a nation doesn't seem so unruly, especially when you look more closely at what they were also meant to accomplish. God knew the Israelites needed laws to benefit them in four other ways.

The laws taught the people that God is holy

The first three of the Ten Commandments addressed people's relationship with God. Much of the 613 laws further expanded on our relationship with God.

> "Speak to the entire assembly of Israel and say to them: 'Be holy because I, the Lord your God, am holy (Lev 19:2).

The 613 laws continued to reveal God's holy character to future generations.

> "Assemble the people—men, women and children, and the foreigners residing in your towns—so they can listen and learn to fear the Lord your God and follow carefully all the words of this law [the 613 laws]. Their children, who do not know this law, must hear it and learn to fear the Lord your God as long as you live in the land you are crossing the Jordan to possess" (Deut 31:12–13; explanation added).

Holiness as part of God's character is clearly indicated in many of the 613 laws about worship and the way in which people were to approach the Lord's presence. The very fact that no one but the High Priest was allowed to enter the Holy of Holies, and thus into the presence of the Lord, points out God's holiness and our humanity in relation to him. There was a clear emphasis on the separation between God's presence and people other than God's appointed priesthood. These laws helped the Israelites (and us) clarify their position in relationship with our holy God.

The laws set his people apart

In giving these laws to the Israelites, God was setting them apart as different from other nations. He told them,

> "Keep my decrees and follow them. I am the LORD, who makes you holy [set apart for a holy purpose]" (Lev 20:8; explanation added).

God wanted other nations to notice his special relationship with the Israelites. The laws of Moses revealed God and his character to other people. People in other nations would know more about God by seeing how the Israelites followed his laws. A people whose character reflects God's character honors him. Others look at what we say, what we do, and what we believe. If those three things align, then people take notice, and our lives have a greater ability to glorify God.

> **To illustrate the point:** Rahab, a prostitute, lived in the town of Jericho. She hid the Jewish spies who had come to check out Jericho's fortifications. In exchange, the Israelites rescued both Rahab and her family when they conquered the city. When Rahab first met the spies, she said, "our hearts melted in fear and everyone's courage failed because of you, for the LORD your God is God in heaven above and on the earth below" (Josh 2:11).
>
> God wanted other nations to notice his special relationship with the Israelites. Rahab noticed, and she wanted to have that special relationship, too.

Those laws were meant to set God's people apart. In our relationship with God, we too are to recognize how he has set us apart for his holy purpose.

The laws created boundaries of behavior for life in a pagan land

God knew that the Jewish people were soon going to enter a land and be surrounded by people who believed in other gods. The Israelites would be susceptible to the influence of those people. A benefit to the Israelites (and us) of the 613 laws, was that they were a way for God to give his chosen people encouragement and guidance as they tried to remain faithful to him while surrounded by ungodly influences.

> **Connection Point**: This sounds a lot like life today. In what ways do you feel susceptible to the influence of other people?

The laws identified sin

The writing down of the 613 laws was completed and then read aloud to the Israelites just before Moses' death over 39 years after God wrote out the Ten Commandments himself on the stone tablets. The Ten Commandments had been placed inside the Ark of the Covenant (Josh 23:6). The 613 laws, however, were placed *next to and outside* of the Ark which contained God's presence.

> "Take this Book of the Law, and put it beside the ark of the covenant of the LORD your God, that it may be there as a witness against you" (Deut 31:26).

Those 613 laws were instructions separate from the Ten Commandments, meant to be simple and help the Israelites set up their new society. The 613 laws, however, were also a witness against the Israelites, by clearly defining what constituted sin, so they could see it in their own lives. The benefit to the Israelites (and us) was that the detailed nature of the laws also helped them (and us) understand our inability to become righteous on our own, preparing the way for Jesus' covenant of grace.[6]

Adding the thousands of man-made rules and regulations

God gave the Israelites simple plans to establish a whole new government and society in only 613 laws, in addition to setting out what they needed

---

6. For more about working for righteousness v. God's covenant of grace, see Appendix G

to know about the priesthood, the Tabernacle, and sacrifices. The laws set out his standards for righteousness to address our human tendency for backsliding. God's laws thus helped define sin as the Apostle Paul explains:

> if it had not been for the law, I would not have known sin (Rom 7:7).

That is essentially what God told Moses when he first dictated the 613 laws. God said the law would be "a witness against you." The law gave the Israelites a standard to live up to so people would recognize when they sinned.

Unfortunately, after Moses wrote down all those God-given laws, Jewish scholars started adding new regulations, requirements, and traditions for the Israelites to follow. The 613 might have been simple, but the thousands of human interpretations made it nearly impossible for people to not break at least a few.

By Jesus' time, the Pharisees (a group of Jewish leaders devoted to an intellectual understanding of the law) had focused not on using the law to help them recognize their own sin but on a need to follow God's laws and the rules, regulations, requirements, and traditions they themselves had added in order to become righteous. They tried to be right with God by what they did—to prove to him they deserved his favor. Unfortunately, that was not how God worked.

> Therefore no one will be declared righteous in God's sight by the works of the law [by working to follow the laws]; rather, through the law we become conscious of our sin (Rom 3:20; explanation added).

It is the breaking of those manmade rules and traditions that the Pharisees used to condemn Jesus.

> Then some Pharisees and teachers of the law came to Jesus from Jerusalem and asked, "Why do your disciples break *the tradition* of the elders? They don't wash their hands before they eat!" (Matt 15:1–2; emphasis added)

Let's see. That might have been Mom's rule in your house when growing up, but where in Scripture does God command people to wash their hands before they eat? That's right. Nowhere. The Pharisees knew that. They were instead referring to tradition; human creation of rules beyond God's law. While washing your hands before eating is a good idea in general, it was not a command by God. It was certainly not required for salvation. Jesus appropriately called them out over their insistence on tradition versus God's commandments, saying

> "And why do you break the command of God for the sake of your tradition?" (Matt 15:3)

Jesus challenged the rules which the Pharisees emphasized, as an unbearable burden on the people. In fact, the burden was so heavy that righteousness was impossible for people to achieve by following rules—even for the Pharisees. The book of Acts addresses this.

> Through him [Jesus] everyone who believes is set free from every sin, a justification you were not able to obtain under the law of Moses (Acts 13:39; explanation added).

We can't make ourselves righteous by obeying the law. The law can show us what sin is so we recognize it in our lives. But the only way we can be right with God is because God chooses to forgive us and chooses to make us right with him by forgiving us when we don't deserve forgiveness. It is through belief in Jesus that we are forgiven and thus made right with God. Righteousness is not achieved by what we do or don't do ourselves, and whether we follow his laws or not. Righteousness is based on our relationship with Jesus.

> So the law was our guardian until Christ came that we might be justified by faith. Now that this faith has come, we are no longer under a guardian (Gal 3: 24–25).

The law was a standard to help identify and define sin. The Pharisees' standard, however, was so high, people tried and failed to achieve that standard. Recognizing our inability to achieve those standards on our own though, prepared us to accept Jesus' gift of salvation. We are saved not by working hard to obey, but through God's grace and forgiveness.

God's plan is simple. He commands us to be righteous. We can't be righteous on our own, so God makes us right with him (righteous) by what *he* did for us—through Jesus' sacrifice. When God the Father sent Jesus, he was doing something new. Something unheard of. Something simple for us. Believe in Jesus and be saved.

Connection Point: Scripture tells us adding to God's rules is a sin.[7] The Pharisees complicated the Israelites' faith with their interpretations and Jesus called them out for doing so. What do you think? If we try to interpret God's plan for our faith in a way that complicates it, is that different from what the Pharisees did?

Chapter Summary

- **Theology Simplified:** All of God's rules are for our benefit. When we live with him as our focus, our lives are better. God's rules weren't complicated until mankind started interpreting them in a way that made it impossible for anyone to obey all of them. It was people, not God, who made a mess of things. Fortunately, God simplified his plan further for us—by having Jesus fulfill the law.

- **What's it to me?** It doesn't seem like all those 613 laws have anything to do with us. But looked at from our modern point of view, imagine if there were only 613 laws in the entire world. Or 613 laws in just our country. Or in your state. Or even in your town. Looking at those laws from that perspective can give you an appreciation of the care God took in creating rules for the Israelites to make their lives better in their new nation and society. It is another way God did something practical to simplify our faith.

- **Faith Simplified:** God gave the Israelites additional rules to establish their nation and help them get along among themselves and with other nations. God's rules were fairly simple until mankind complicated them.

This is the third of five principles of *Faith Simplified* which this book is based on: God's rules are for our benefit.

---

7. Prov 30:5–6; Deut 4:2; 12:32

Principle 4

How Did Jesus Fulfill the Law
and What Does that Mean?

10

Jesus Fulfilled the Law

"Do not think that I have come to abolish the Law or the Prophets; I have not come to abolish them but to fulfill them" (Matt 5:17).

WE HEAR THIS VERSE in church from time to time. We may have caught an entire sermon on it. We think, great! All those laws are gone forever. Thank you, Jesus!

Yes, thank you, Jesus! But that verse doesn't actually say Jesus got rid of those laws. In fact, it says, he didn't abolish them at all. What's going on?

The problem with the laws

God dictated just 613 laws to Moses to establish the priesthood, the Tabernacle, and the sacrificial system and simplify how the Israelites were to set up a new government and society in the Promised Land. In the grand scheme of things, 613 laws for all those purposes wasn't very many at all. By the time Jesus began his earthly ministry, however, Jewish religious leaders (especially the sect of Pharisees who were regarded as experts in the laws of Moses) had added thousands of interpretations, rules, regulations, and traditions to those simple ones God had dictated. Those thousands became so cumbersome, it was impossible for people to understand or remember them all, much less obey them.

The Apostle Paul, originally a Pharisee himself, addressed the rules the Pharisees thought were so important by pointing out that trying to follow them perfectly was like trying to prove to God that we are righteous on our own, which we are not.[1] Fortunately, Jesus' life, death, and resurrection brought about a new covenant between God and man. Essentially, being right with God became about having a right relationship with God the Father by first having a relationship with Jesus. In fact, Jesus told us: "The work of God is this: to believe in the one he has sent" (John 6:29). Christians often say they want to do God's work; they want to do his will; to know his calling for them. Jesus has already answered the question of what it means for us to do the work of God. All we have to do is believe in Jesus—that is God's will for us. That is God's calling to us.

While Jesus' New Covenant is truly better for us, ignoring the Old Covenant and all that God said and did over mankind's history, takes away from the impact of what Jesus accomplished. It also fails to remind us of God's consistency and trustworthiness. While Jesus did institute a new covenant of grace, God has always desired to show his children grace. So let's look at what effect Jesus had on God's laws in the Old Testament.

Jesus did not abolish the laws

Jesus tells us plainly that he did not abolish them. Look at Matthew 5:17 again.

> "Do not think that I have come to abolish the Law or the Prophets;
> I have not come to abolish them but to fulfill them."

For Greater Depth

> The original Greek word used for *fulfill* in Matthew 5:17 is *pleroo*. In that specific verse it means to accomplish, adding to that meaning to fill out, to complete, to make perfect. Applying those meanings, Jesus accomplished what he came to do: to fill out the laws so that they are complete and made perfect, by what he did.[2]

1. Phil 3:9; Rom 3:10; Eccl 7:20; Ps 14:3; Isa 64:6
2. Zodhiates, *Dictionary*, 1177–1178

Paul later expanded on Jesus' remark, saying

> Christ is the *culmination* of the law so that there may be righteousness for everyone who believes (Rom 10:4; emphasis added).

For Greater Depth

> The original Greek word used for *culmination* in Romans 10:4 is *telos*. Its meaning incorporates goal; not simply an ending.[3]

God's standard of righteousness has never changed. Jesus' goal while on earth was to fulfill the Father's demand for righteousness as set out in the law. Because Jesus is ultimate righteousness, the Father sees us as righteous when we claim for ourselves what Jesus accomplished on our behalf. The Holy Spirit working in us, then places those standards of righteousness relevant to our right relationship with God in our hearts. The Holy Spirit, not the written law, now teaches us about righteousness, what that means, and how to live.

There is another way that Jesus fulfilled the laws without abolishing them. Earlier we categorized the group of 613 laws as laws relating to God and laws relating to the world. Let's look at those two categories again with Jesus' fulfillment in mind.

Jesus fulfilled the laws relating to God: priesthood, the Temple, sacrifice

Priesthood

Back in the desert, God selected the tribe of Levi to be the only tribe from all twelve tribes of Israel to be in charge of spiritual matters. A hierarchy was formed within that priesthood with a single individual man from the tribe of Levi appointed as High Priest.[4] Only very select men, sometimes

---

3. Zodhiates, *Dictionary*, 1376–1378

4. See the book of Leviticus generally for rules involving duties and responsibilities of the High Priest. See additional verses about Jesus as High Priest seated with the Father:

Principle 4 | How Did Jesus Fulfill the Law

chosen by lot (similar to dice) to be High Priest, were allowed within the very holiest part of the Temple (called variously the Sanctuary, the Holy of Holies, the Most Holy Place) which contained the Ark of the Covenant. It was only that selected High Priest who could enter the presence of God. The New Testament tells us that Jesus became our High Priest.

For Greater Depth

Specifically, the New Testament says Jesus became our High Priest, in the order of Melchizedek (Heb 5:10). Who in the world was that priest with the impossible name? Melchizedek (pronounced mehl-KIHZ-eh-dehk) was a High Priest mentioned in the Old Testament.[5] He and Jesus shared many characteristics.

- Melchizedek was not a high priest in the Levitical order. Neither was Jesus, who was born into the tribe of Judah.
- Both Melchizedek and eternal Jesus existed before Israel (Jacob) was born.
- Melchizedek was both a king and a priest. Jesus was born through the kingly line of David and is our High Priest.
- Melchizedek means "king of righteousness." He was King of Salem which means "king of peace" (Heb 7:1–3). Scripture refers to Jesus as king of peace and king of righteousness.[6]

That's interesting, you say, but if Jesus is outside of the Levitical order, how can he be our High Priest? Scripture explains.

> Every high priest is selected from among the people and is appointed to represent the people in matters related to God, to offer gifts and sacrifices for sins (Heb 5:1).

Hebrews further explains,

> If perfection could have been attained through the Levitical priesthood—and indeed the law given to the people established that

---

Ps 110:1; Matt 26:64; Mark 14:62; 16:19; Luke 20:42; 22:69; Acts 2:33; 5:31; 7:55; Rom 8:34; Heb 1:3, 13; 8:1–2; 10:12–13; 12:2; Col 3:1; Eph 1:20; 1 Pet 3:22; Rev 3:21

5. Gen 14:18–20; Ps 110:4
6. Isa 9:6–7; 2 Thess 3:16

priesthood—why was there still need for another priest to come, one in the order of Melchizedek, not in the order of Aaron [in other words, not from the Levitical priestly line]? For when the priesthood is changed, the law must be changed also [changed; not abolished] (Heb 7:11–12; explanation added).

No longer do we need a human High Priest to deal with God on our behalf. Now we can deal directly with Jesus. We now have access to the Father because Jesus has access—sitting there as High Priest at the right hand of God the Father.[7] Jesus as our High Priest means several things:

- Just as the only way to the Father for the Jews before Jesus' time was through a human High Priest, now the way to the Father is through Jesus, our eternal High Priest, as Jesus said, "No one comes to the Father except through me" (John 14:6).
- Access to God the Father is immediate and efficient. Jesus tells us that he and the Father are one. Therefore, we can go directly to the source—to God himself—Jesus.[8]
- Access to the Father is relational. We approach God the Father through Jesus, yet we are always in God's presence because the Holy Spirit is within us.
- Before Jesus, only a Levitical High Priest was allowed to be in the holy presence of God within the Holy of Holies inside the Tabernacle (Temple). When we receive the Holy Spirit, we can be continuously in the holy presence of God as the Holy Spirit dwells in us—wherever we are. Scripture tells us that we are now the temple of the Holy Spirit. We are the temple of God.
- Jesus is mediator of the New Covenant. Only a High Priest in the Jewish religious system could deal (mediate, intervene) with God on behalf of people. Jesus is now our mediator. Jesus deals with God the Father on our behalf.

More than all of the above, Jesus is also guarantor of the New Covenant. A guarantor is a person who promises (guarantees) to pay a borrower's debt if the borrower defaults (fails to pay; evades payment). It is

---

7. See additional verses about Jesus as High Priest seated with the Father: Ps 110:1; Matt 26:64; Mark 14:62; 16:19; Luke 20:42; 22:69; Acts 2:33; 5:31; 7:55; Rom 8:34; Heb 1:3, 13; 8:1–2; 10:12–13; 12:2; Col 3:1; Eph 1:20; 1 Pet 3:22; Rev 3:21

8. See John 1:1; 10:30; 14:10

like a co-signer on a loan who agrees to pay off the loan if the person who wants the loan can't or doesn't make the payments. Jesus worked out the New Covenant between the Father and us and then guaranteed our part in the agreement by paying off our entire debt to the Father through his blood sacrifice. It is like you paying off the loan for the person you co-signed for before the signature ink even dried. Jesus mediates on our behalf before God and guarantees that we are recipients of that covenant—if we choose him.

> The Lord has sworn and will not change his mind: "You are a priest forever." Because of this oath, Jesus has become the guarantor of a better covenant (Heb 7:21–22; emphasis added).

The Old Covenant was a two-party agreement. God's part was that if we obeyed him, he would bless us. Our part was to obey him. The New Covenant is God's promise that we are saved not because of what we do or don't do but because of what Jesus did. When we accept what Jesus did for us, we accept this new two-party agreement. God agrees to give us salvation; we agree to accept what Jesus already did. Jesus, as God, has already guaranteed his part of the agreement by dying on the cross as a sacrifice to forgive our sins.

Jesus fulfilled the law of Moses as it related to the priesthood, going beyond what a human High Priest could do.

> **Connection Point**: Imagine not feeling as if you could talk directly with God. Imagine if you had to ask a priest to deal with God on your behalf. How would that make you feel? How do you feel knowing you can approach God directly?

The Tabernacle/Temple

Today we have freedom to worship God whenever and wherever we wish and in whatever way we believe best honors him. We are free to worship with other people on Saturday or Sunday or any other day. We are also free to not worship with other people at all, but to simply worship him in private.

Part of freedom of worship has to do with what Jesus did relating to the Temple. The only place God specified for worship in the 613 laws was

Jesus Fulfilled the Law

the Tabernacle (and later the Temple in Jerusalem).[9] Over time, the Jewish people built local synagogues as places of prayer and study,[10] but the Temple in Jerusalem was the place to worship. It was where sacrifices were made. It was where God's presence resided—specifically within the Holy of Holies.

The Holy of Holies was separated from the rest of the Temple (and earlier, the Tabernacle) by a curtain. At the moment Jesus died on the cross, the curtain separating the Holy of Holies and the rest of the Temple was torn in half.[11] Physically and symbolically, mankind no longer had to be separated from God's presence. Therefore worship was no longer limited to the Temple. The physical Temple in Jerusalem has since been destroyed. That means worship in the Temple is no longer even possible.

Jesus explained this new freedom of worship. At the well, the Samaritan woman asked if people should worship at the Temple in Jerusalem or at Mount Shiloh in Samaria where the original Tabernacle had been located.

> "Woman," Jesus replied, "believe me, a time is coming when you will worship the Father neither on this mountain nor in Jerusalem" (John 4:21).

Then Jesus added,

> "Yet a time is coming and has now come when the true worshipers will worship the Father in the Spirit and in truth, for they are the kind of worshipers the Father seeks" (John 4:23).

In other words, it no longer matters where you worship. The important part of worship is to worship in the Spirit and in truth. God's presence—through the indwelling of the Holy Spirit—resides within us. We believers are now the Temple of the Lord (1 Cor 6:19). By sending the Holy Spirit to dwell in us, Jesus fulfilled the law of Moses as it related to the Temple. Wherever we are now is the perfect place for worship and we worship in the Spirit. Notice the capital S in John 4:23? We don't worship in or through our spirit (little s). We worship in or through the Spirit; God's Spirit; the Holy Spirit in us, because there is connection, intimate union, oneness of heart, mind, and purpose.[12]

---

9. See Deut 12:5; 12:11–14

10. Luke 4:16; 13:10; Mark 1:21; Acts 18:4

11. Matt 27:51; Mark 15:38; Luke 23:45

12. Zodhiates, *Dictionary*, 579–583 more than four pages discuss the complex implications of the tiny Greek word *en* (meaning *in*)

Connection Point: In your personal worship, do you feel closer to God inside a church building, on a mountain top, at the ocean? How do you feel knowing you can worship God at any time and any place because the Holy Spirit is with you at all times?

Sin and blood sacrifice

According to the 613 laws, every sin required a specific, unique, and separate blood sacrifice to cover that sin. If you look at the book of Leviticus carefully, it's as if God is saying "There is nothing you can do that I haven't created a way for you to come back to me."

While that is a wonderful example of how much God loves us, the process was astonishingly complicated. The description of the sacrifice for the Day of Atonement, for example, is presented in detail, taking up the entire Chapter 16 in the book of Leviticus. The ceremony was intricate and complex, involving five separate animals. Even so, the complicated ceremony and accompanying animal sacrifices were still insufficient to cover all sins of all people for all time.

Jesus' blood, as we saw, was sufficient to forgive all sins for all people forever.[13] Thus, Jesus fulfilled the law as it related to sin and blood sacrifice.

> **To illustrate the point:** Imagine if life today continued with the sacrificial system God had dictated to Moses long ago. We would still be sinning. And every time we sinned, we would have to go to a priest and ask him to sacrifice an animal so our sin could be covered, although never entirely forgiven. Would we have to keep a flock of sheep and goats in our backyard to have sacrifices on hand for ourselves and our family? God's laws say we can only worship at his Temple—the one that now lies in shambles.
>
> "Grab your hiking boots," the wife would say. "Dad is waiting in the car. Then it's a long trip on the plane and a bumpy drive to Jerusalem!"
>
> You would have to carefully obey all of God's 613 laws in addition to the Big Ten. Otherwise, you could not be right with God. Scripture tells us to write God's laws on our doorframes. You'd need a really big doorframe.

---

13. Many people wonder about the unforgivable sin—blasphemy of the Holy Spirit. See Appendix H for a short explanation of what blasphemy is and why it is unforgivable.

You would do a lot of sighing, a lot of trying again, and a lot of asking for God's help in obeying those laws. You would also do a lot of hoping that God saw your obedience and would judge it as enough.

Jesus did not abolish the law. The need for a blood sacrifice of an innocent never stopped being one of God's requirements to deal with our sins. God does not change. He is still trustworthy to keep his covenants. God set up the rules and hasn't changed them. God however, dramatically simplified things for us—by taking care of fulfilling his requirements by what Jesus—God himself—did. When Jesus provided the sacrifice of himself, he fulfilled the law of Moses as it related to the sacrificial system.

> **Connection Point**: It's hard for us to comprehend the extent of sacrifices made in the ancient world. Even though those sacrificed animals were ultimately used as food, how would you feel if you knew that the lambchop you were munching on was from a lamb who had died because of something you did personally?

Jesus fulfilled the law about our place in the world

Many of the 613 laws set out to establish a government and society, with rules for daily life of a large community on the move, ready to establish itself in a new land. The intent was for the Israelites to live together in harmony among themselves and with neighboring pagan people.

Dietary rules

One of the aspects of those regulations that puzzle modern people are God's dietary requirements. Many scholars assume the farming and animal raising standards at the time required such rules to keep God's people healthy until they settled and their food base became established. Whatever the reason for those dietary laws, in the early years of Jewish society, God determined a need for them. The need was so great, that eating or even touching certain foods made a person unclean and thus unacceptable to God. Being unclean then required action (sometimes a sacrifice) by the priests to cover the sin of the touching or eating prohibited foods.

Principle 4 | How Did Jesus Fulfill the Law

Once Jesus died, grace took the place of restrictive behavior. After Jesus' sacrifice, one of the freedoms God granted us was freedom over what we could eat. Eating previously prohibited things was no longer a sin that had to be covered—because all sin was forgiven by Jesus' sacrifice in the first place. Moreover, Jesus declared that all foods were "clean."

> "Don't you see that nothing that enters a person from the outside can defile them? For it doesn't go into their heart but into their stomach, and then out of the body." (In saying this, Jesus declared all foods clean.)[14]

To illustrate the point: Imagine an ancient Jewish man transported to the modern world. He takes a bite of a hot dog from the vendor on the corner. "This is delicious!" he says. "What is it?"

"A bit of beef, some chicken. Mostly pork," the hot dog vendor replies.

"Pork?" the man hurls the hot dog into the garbage and wipes his hands on his cloak frantically. "I have eaten an unclean animal!" he says. "Where is the Temple? Where can I offer a sacrifice and beg the priest to ask God to cover my sin?"

"Hang on, brother," the hot dog vendor says. "Let me tell you about Jesus."

The Jewish man listens. He leans closer to the vendor. He takes a step forward. "You mean," says the man, "Jesus fulfilled all those laws so we can eat anything we want? You mean Jesus fulfilled all those laws so we can worship right here; right now?"

The hot dog vendor nods. "All you have to do is believe in Jesus. When you do, he covers you with grace. He forgives your sins. He promises you eternal life with him in Heaven."

"Even if I eat hot dogs?" the man asks. "God can even forgive that?"

"I wouldn't sell 'em if I couldn't eat 'em," the vendor replies. "Do you believe?"

The man pauses. "I'd be a fool not to accept what Jesus did. Yes, I sure do choose to believe!"

"Amen, brother!" says the vendor, handing the man another hot dog. "On the house."

---

14. Mark 7:18–19; explanation in original; later confirmed by Peter in Acts 10:11–15

The vendor picks up a bottle of mustard. "You'll want some of this with that. Made from the tiniest seed in the garden, but it really packs a punch. Jesus liked mustard, too. Let me tell you a story."

"I'm listening," says the Jewish man, shoving the hot dog into his mouth.

The Bible makes it clear that "the kingdom of God is not a matter of eating and drinking, but of righteousness, peace and joy in the Holy Spirit" (Rom 14:17), adding that there is no salvation in either eating or not eating certain foods. Rather we are saved by grace through faith in the Lord Jesus Christ (Eph 2:8–10), knowing that whenever we eat or drink, we are to do it in a way that honors the Lord (1 Cor 10:31).

Jesus also fulfilled the dietary laws spiritually. Scripture tells us that man does not live on bread alone but on every word that comes from the mouth of God (Deut 8:3). In furtherance of this thinking, Jesus told us that blessed are those who hunger and thirst for righteousness (Matt 5:6). When we hunger and thirst after righteousness, we are satisfied by the word of God and by seeking to be made right with God (righteous) through Jesus.

Jesus also fulfilled the dietary laws symbolically, by reminding us what he did for us on the cross. We are to eat bread, remembering his body broken for us, when he took on our sins. We are to drink wine, remembering his blood shed for us, representing forgiveness of those sins. Jesus referred to himself as the bread of life from Heaven and as living water.[15] Symbolically, Jesus reminds us that he fulfilled the old dietary laws.

The old dietary laws were not abolished. Rather Jesus fulfilled them—giving us grace in our free will decisions over food and also providing exactly what we need to satisfy our hunger and thirst for righteousness—knowing him.

> **Connection Point**: We have grace for however we honor God through what we eat and drink. Many modern people follow the Old Testament dietary laws as a way to honor Jesus. Do you? Or do you honor him by rejoicing that he fulfilled those laws?

---

15. John 6:35; 7:37–38

Relationships

Jesus fulfilled the law by showing us what the law means as it relates to others. In our relationships with other people, we are to value them. We are not to think ourselves better than others. We are to serve others. We are to be kind in our approach to others.

Additionally, when we are wronged, we are not to seek vengeance or retaliation. In the Old Testament, each sin had a specific consequence. Jesus, however, instituted a new system of grace.

> Make sure that nobody pays back wrong for wrong, but always strive to do what is good for each other and for everyone else.[16]

In other words, just as God forgives us, we are to follow his example and forgive others. We are to pray for God's guidance. We are to pray for others; even for our enemies. We are always to put God's will above our own. We are to stand up for what is right, however, even if it results in conflict. We are also to do good for other people, even if they have wronged us.

Connection Point: Imagine living in a society based on a strict eye for an eye judgment. How would you feel if God pursued eye for an eye judgment? Are you glad he doesn't?

Jesus' life, death, and resurrection dealt with the many, detailed laws about everyday life and relationships with others. Jesus fulfilled the law by showing how God wants us to live. Then he left us with the Holy Spirit, to remind us of his teachings (John 14:26) and further simplify the process for us.

Jesus fulfilled the writing of the prophets: The New Covenant

Let's return to the verse we started this chapter with:

> "Do not think that I have come to abolish the Law or the Prophets; I have not come to abolish them but to fulfill them" (Matt 5:17).

In addition to the law, Jesus said he came to fulfill the prophets (their writings or what they said). The book of Hebrews summarized Jesus'

---

16. 1 Thess 5:15; see additional verses about relationships: Zech 7:9–10; Ps 82:3–4; 72:4; Jer 5:28; 22:3; Prov 21:13; 22:16; Jas 1:27; 4:17; 1 John 3:17–18

fulfillment of the law by reminding us what God said through the prophet Jeremiah.

> "The days are coming, declares the Lord, when I will make a new covenant with the people of Israel and with the people of Judah" (Heb 8:8, referencing Jeremiah; emphasis added).

Hebrews then continues.

> This is the covenant I will establish with the people of Israel after that time, declares the Lord. I will put my laws in their minds and write them on their hearts. I will be their God, and they will be my people. No longer will they teach their neighbor, or say to one another, 'Know the Lord,' because they will all know me, from the least of them to the greatest. For I will forgive their wickedness and will remember their sins no more" (Heb 8:10–12, quoting Jer 31:33–34; emphasis added).

At least 600 years before Jesus' birth, God told Jeremiah he would make a new covenant, putting his laws in our minds and hearts and forgiving our wickedness. Jesus accomplished the putting the laws in our minds and hearts by sending the Holy Spirit to further teach and remind us of these things. And Jesus' sacrifice enabled God to forgive our wickedness. Jesus fulfilled what God had said he would do through the writings of the prophets.

Jesus' New Covenant thus made the Old Covenant outdated.

> By calling this covenant "new," he has made the first one obsolete (Heb 8:13).

The Old Covenant was not abolished (done away with; obliterated; destroyed). Rather, after Jesus fulfilled the Old Covenant, it was simply no longer applicable (relevant; pertinent). It was obsolete (outdated; outmoded; antiquated). So it was superseded (supplanted; updated; reworked); by a new and better covenant, which had been part of God's plan from the beginning.

> **To illustrate the point:** Imagine you have a one-year lease agreement on a home. The owner of the home signs the agreement; you, as the renter sign the agreement. Later you and the owner of the home make a new agreement. You agree to make higher monthly payments and the owner agrees to apply part of those payments toward your future purchase of the home. That new

agreement, signed by both parties, is the one now in effect and which both parties must honor.

At the end of the year-long term of the original lease agreement, the physical paper agreement which both parties signed, is sitting in a file in the owner's desk. Your copy of that original agreement is somewhere in a pile of papers in your cardboard box, labeled "Important." That original agreement still exists, but it is no longer relevant. It will not be enforced because the new Lease to Own Agreement has become the agreement both parties honor.

Before he died on the cross, Jesus said, "It is finished" (John 19:30)—not just his earthly life; not just his sacrifice; but completion of all of God's plan to offer salvation to us, including fulfilling the law and the writings of the prophets. God's part of the New Covenant was done. Our part of the covenant is up to us—saying "yes" to Jesus' gift.

Connection Point: Imagine having to obey every Old Testament law, knowing that if you didn't, you had to cover that sin of disobedience with a blood sacrifice. It's exhausting, just thinking about how easy it would be to miss a law; or worse, not really care some days because the process was so tedious and so exhausting to keep up with.

Chapter Summary

- **Theology Simplified:** God consistently wants us to obey his laws. But the grace given us through Jesus took the place of restrictive behavior as a requirement for being right with God. Now, God's laws are written in our minds and hearts, just as God planned before Jesus' earthly ministry began. Now we are made righteous (right with God) through our relationship with Jesus.

- **What's it to me?** The most obvious benefit is that you no longer have to check off obedience to all those laws or even know what they are. The Holy Spirit will teach and remind you about the ones you need to know, when you need to know them. This is one more example of how

Jesus Fulfilled the Law

God continues to simplify your part of faith. He keeps making it easier and easier to love him.

- **Faith Simplified:** Obedience didn't bring the Israelites salvation so Jesus established a new, easier-to-follow covenant. Now, to be right with God, all we need to do is believe in Jesus.

11

God Simplified the Law into Two Rules

WHEN JESUS WAS ALIVE on earth, the Pharisees were busily enforcing thousands of rules beyond the ones God had dictated to Moses. One day, one of those experts in the law asked Jesus which commandment was greatest. Jesus responded.

> "'Love the Lord your God with all your heart and with all your soul and with all your mind and with all your strength.' The second is this: 'Love your neighbor as yourself.' There is no commandment greater than these" (Mark 12:30–31).

Two commandments. Two simple rules to make our lives good. Love God. Love others.

At first, we might think Jesus had merely combined the first three of the Ten Commandments when he talked about loving God. After our study of the Ten Commandments, however, we know that those three commandments deal with respecting God. They don't say anything about loving him. Since Jesus didn't misquote Scripture, what was he doing when he responded to the expert in the law that we are to love God?

The Gospel accounts of Matthew, Mark, and Luke

The Gospel accounts of Matthew, Mark, and Luke, confirm what Jesus said about the greatest commandments. Here are the three accounts so you can compare them.

From Matthew:

God Simplified the Law into Two Rules

> Hearing that Jesus had silenced the Sadducees, the Pharisees got together. One of them, an expert in the law, tested him with this question: "Teacher, which is the greatest commandment in the Law?"
>
> Jesus replied: "'Love the Lord your God with all your heart and with all your soul and with all your mind.' This is the first and greatest commandment. And the second is like it: 'Love your neighbor as yourself'" (Matt 22:34–39).

From Mark:

> [Jesus speaking] "'Love the Lord your God with all your heart and with all your soul and with all your mind and with all your strength.
>
> "The second is this: 'Love your neighbor as yourself.' There is no commandment greater than these."
>
> "Well said, teacher," the man replied. "You are right in saying that God is one and there is no other but him. To love him with all your heart, with all your understanding and with all your strength, and to love your neighbor as yourself is more important than all burnt offerings and sacrifices" (Mark 12:30–33; explanation added).

From Luke:

> "What is written in the Law?" he [Jesus] replied. "How do you read it?"
>
> He [the expert in the law] answered, "'Love the Lord your God with all your heart and with all your soul and with all your strength and with all your mind'; and, 'Love your neighbor as yourself.'"
>
> "You have answered correctly," Jesus replied. "Do this and you will live" (Luke 10:26–28; explanation added).

First, let's note a couple of minor variations in the accounts of the three Gospels. While Matthew confirms Jesus said to love God with our heart, soul, and mind, he did not include loving God with our strength. Luke records the expert in the law quoting Scripture and Jesus confirming it. Mark records Jesus quoting the Scripture and the expert confirming what Jesus said.

Despite these minor variations, all three Gospel accounts are consistent in the message: both Jesus and the expert in the law agree that the two greatest commandments are to love God and to love others.

Principle 4 | How Did Jesus Fulfill the Law

Where did Jesus come up with those commandments?

That expert in the law of Moses was well versed not only in the Ten Commandments, but also in the 613 laws and the thousands of man-interpreted regulations. He would have known if Jesus had just made up something new. But he never contradicted Jesus.

> **To illustrate the point:** Imagine it's 32 AD. You're standing on a street corner in Jerusalem listening to Jesus. An expert in the law approaches. You've seen him around the Temple—Benjamin is his name. A Pharisee. You know why he's here. He's trying to trap Jesus; make him say something the Pharisees could arrest him for.
>
> Should you warn Jesus? you wonder. No, Jesus has this. So you listen.
>
> "Teacher," Benjamin asks, "which is the most important of all of God's laws?"
>
> You hear his question and remember that God had 613 laws and the Pharisees had added thousands of rules to those original laws. What would Jesus say? Which law would Jesus choose? There are so many.
>
> You see Jesus look Benjamin in the eyes and smile. You've been following Jesus now long enough to know what he must have been thinking. Probably something like, "You're the expert in the law. Why are you asking me? You should know this."
>
> But instead, you hear Jesus reply, "The most important law is to love God with all your heart, all your soul, all your mind, and all your strength."
>
> Benjamin nods slightly, looking surprised. Then Jesus continues, "There is another law that is just as important. It is to love your neighbor as yourself."
>
> "You quote from the books of Moses!" Benjamin follows Jesus into the Temple, nearly tripping over the stones as he tries to keep up. "Teacher you know your Scripture!"
>
> Love God, love others. Jesus has done it again, you think. He made things so simple for us. You follow Jesus into the Temple.

When Jesus replied with the first and greatest commandment, he knew he was speaking with an expert in the law who knew and had studied

God Simplified the Law into Two Rules

all of them. So Jesus responded by quoting law the expert was familiar with. Jesus first quoted from Deuteronomy, one of the books referred to by the Jews as containing the law of Moses.

> Love the Lord your God with all your heart and with all your soul and with all your strength (Deut 6:5).

Then Jesus quoted from Leviticus, another of the books referred to by the Jews as containing the law of Moses.

> love your neighbor as yourself (Lev 19:18).

Jesus put those two commandments from the books of Moses together for the expert in the law, saying

> "Love the Lord your God with all your heart and with all your soul and with all your mind and with all your strength.' The second is this: 'Love your neighbor as yourself.' There is no commandment greater than these."[1]

Then Jesus added the clincher in Matthew:

> "All the Law and the Prophets hang on these two commandments (Matt 22:40; emphasis added).

Jesus simplified all of the hundreds of laws; all of the thousands of regulations into just two. All of the law and everything the prophets had ever tried to tell people on behalf of God, hang on those two commandments.

Love God. Love others. Two rules; four words. God continues to simplify our part of his plan. The first three of the Ten Commandments have to do with our relationship with God. The last six commandments have to do with our relationship with others. Commandment Four addresses both relationships. The simplicity of Jesus' two commandments encompasses all of them.

How though are we supposed to love God with our heart, our soul, our mind, and our strength?

> **Connection Point**: Were you aware that Jesus was quoting Scripture when he stated the two greatest commandments? How do you feel knowing that those two existed even before Jesus' earthly life?

---

1. Mark 12:30–31; see also Matt 22:37–39; Luke 10:27

Principle 4 | How Did Jesus Fulfill the Law

Chapter Summary

- **Theology Simplified:** God's Ten Commandments, along with his 613 laws were simple and good. But they had been made burdensome by the religious scholars. Two thousand years later, Jesus basically said, "You already know how to run a nation and live a good life and I will take care of everything dealing with your relationship with God. Now all you need to remember is this: Love God and love others."

- **What's it to me?** You might be able to recite all of the Ten Commandments. Maybe even in order. But isn't it a lot easier to remember just two? Jesus even put those two into the proper perspective. You are first to love God. By having a right relationship with God and understanding how he loves you, you can then extend that love with other people. It's not a matter of loving God *more* than you love your spouse or your children or your friend. It's a matter of loving God in a different, deeper, more profound way. We'll look at that next.

- **Faith Simplified:** Jesus simplified all the laws for us into just two: love God and love others.

12

Love God with All Your Heart, Soul, Mind, and Strength

THE SIMPLE POINT TO remember in this chapter is this: Love God with everything you are. When we think about putting that simple point into practice, however, we stress over it. What does it actually mean to love God with my heart? How do I love God with my soul? I'm not even sure what my soul is. How can my mind love? Whatever does strength have to do with loving God? Surely God is not implying I spend my life at the gym.

Let's look at each of the locations (where or place within us or the mechanism to use) to love God, always remembering the underlying simple point: Love God with everything you are.

First, love God with your heart

In modern times, we interpret the phrase "love with your heart" as emotional love. Things are heart-felt. Things touch our hearts emotionally. Something heart-breaking is sad. The modern thinking is that emotions reside within our hearts. That definition, however, does not reflect the *where* we are to love God.

For Greater Depth

> The Hebrew word for *heart*, as used in the Old Testament is *lebab*. It refers to understanding. The definition does not generally include an element of emotions, although emotions are not entirely discounted in the definition. The primary use of this word describes the entire nature of "the inner person that God can discern."[1]

Often, our emotions bubble up haphazardly in our lives. Emotions may be swayed by what is going on around us. Emotions come and go. Emotions are unreliable. Not surprisingly then, the biblical definition of heart does not imply that we are to first love God emotionally. Loving God goes deeper than emotional love. It goes beyond the surface of what is happening in our lives.

Heart comes first in the sequence of ways we are to love him. If we believe God doesn't do things randomly, then heart is first for a reason. Taking into account the above biblical definition of heart as a place of understanding, the instruction Jesus quoted from Deuteronomy has to do with rational thinking, not emotion. Most biblical scholars looking at the Hebrew word *lebab* relate it to an intellectual, decision-making response to God at our innermost level.

We modern folk associate *heart* with the location of our physical heart—in the center of our chest. But ancient folk thought of the heart in the spiritual context as "the gut." Put in terms we can understand, when presented with the existence and character of God, something deep inside us—at a gut level—reacts instinctively yet intellectually. "Yes! I recognize that God is worthy" our gut says. "Therefore I will love him!" In other words, the logical sequence to first making a decision for Jesus in the heart (gut) is: Instinctive recognition of the evidence. Then make the intellectual decision to love God.

Scripture tells us the heart is the dwelling place of God. We are told that the Holy Spirit lives in the hearts of the believer. Christ dwells in our hearts.

---

1. Baker, *Dictionary*, 537

> Because you are his sons, God sent the Spirit of his Son into our hearts, the Spirit who calls out, "*Abba*, Father" (Gal 4:6; emphasis in original).

Here's another verse about God dwelling in our hearts.

> And hope does not put us to shame, because God's love has been poured out into our hearts through the Holy Spirit, who has been given to us (Rom 5:5).

Here's another verse.

> Christ may dwell in your hearts through faith (Eph 3:17).

For some of us, it is easier to think of our gut as our inmost being. It's certainly more spiritual sounding than *gut*. *Inmost being* is also a phrase used occasionally in Scripture. For example:

> The human spirit is the lamp of the LORD that sheds light on one's inmost being (Prov 20:27).

Interestingly, the King James version of this verse uses the term *inner part of the belly* instead of *inmost being*. The "inner part of the belly" sounds a lot like what we think of as *gut*.

For Greater Depth

> The Hebrew word for belly is *beten*. *Beten* refers to the inner being of a person; where the spiritual being expresses itself.[2]

Whether the spiritual heart refers to our physical one or some nonphysical place within us, our decision for God is made first there—in the heart at a gut level. God then dwells there in our hearts through the Holy Spirit. The Holy Spirit teaches us about God and directs and counsels us. Therefore, it is rational to love God first with our hearts.

To illustrate the point: A friend was at the hospital awaiting his first child. He hadn't thought too much about how he would react to the child. He was certainly nervous about the responsibility. He was worried about his wife during the delivery. He figured

2. Baker, *Dictionary*, 129

he would eventually grow to love the child, but babies? Hang on to them for a few years, he thought. I'll catch up with them when they turn into real people.

Then the nurse placed his infant daughter in his arms. He looked at that tiny face, so new and precious. How he loved his child! He felt that love deep in his gut. Instinctively he wanted to protect her. Instinctively he loved her. Instinctively he felt as if his heart would break when he released her back to the nurse.

Other people love baby animals. I pull to the side of the road to watch baby goats frolic. A puppy has the power to soften even the grumpiest heart. A newborn colt gives us awe-filled joy. These are instinctive reactions. We feel them in our inmost being. That gut level love is what we are to have for God. It is instinctive and intellectual, felt in the deepest part of who we are.

Remember: We are to love God with everything we are.

Connection Point: Do you think you love God with your heart? How might you think differently about "loving God with your heart" in light of your new understanding of the original Hebrew word used in Scripture?

Second, love God with your soul

We often think of soul and spirit as one and the same. But the Bible clearly tells us they are different.

> For the word of God is alive and active. Sharper than any double-edged sword, it penetrates even to *dividing soul and spirit*.[3]

What is soul? What is spirit?

We wonder what the difference is between soul and spirit and how does that relate to loving God?

---

3. Heb 4:12; emphasis added; see also 1 Thess 5:23

For Greater Depth

> The Greek word for *soul* is *psuches*. *Psuches* refers to the immortal part of man. It is the non-physical part of a person; our personality, our ability to put facts together, our intellect, our feelings, the individual person we are.[4]

The immortal, non-physical part of who you are—that's your soul. Biblically, your soul is the eternal you. It is your personality, your talents, your inclinations, what makes you unique and individual. It is how God specifically created you to be the person you are. Your soul is also eternal. It is what lives on after your physical death. Jesus said,

> Do not be afraid of those who kill the body but cannot kill the soul. Rather, be afraid of the One who can destroy both soul and body in hell" (Matthew 10:28).

We don't have a soul. We *are* a soul. We *have* a body. Or, put another way, we are an eternal soul with a mortal body.

The essence of a believer in Christ (the soul; who we are) does not die when the body dies. The soul is not just some wisp of smokey vapor. The soul is eternal. It goes somewhere after death when it (who we are) is released from our physical body. A believer's soul goes to Heaven; a non-believer's soul does not. Our soul is what Jesus came to save. It is what Satan fights to own.

In addition to a soul, everyone has an impersonal force called a "spirit."

For Greater Depth

> The Greek word for spirit is *pneuma*. It is defined by its attribute. The human spirit is what gives a person the ability to communicate with God's Spirit.[5]

As defined above, our spirit is a *what*; not a *who*.

---

4. Zodhiates, *Dictionary*, 1491–1495
5. Zodhiates, *Dictionary*, 1118–1186

Looking at soul and spirit together, we recognize that our soul is who we are as an individual. Our soul lives forever. Our spirit on the other hand, is not who we are. Our spirit is an impersonal God-given ability or pathway for communication with God. Did you get that? God gave us a pathway—our spirit—as a way to communicate with him. Here. On earth. Through prayer. With the Holy Spirit's guidance.

But how do those definitions of soul and spirit work together to explain how we relate to God? We know that God does not create evil. Rather, while God created our soul as the unique individual we are, He created it as spiritually neutral, or balanced, or like a blank slate as it relates to good and evil. Thus, our soul starts out as sinless. But there's that asterisk from Adam and Eve's sin, reminding us of our tendency to sin. We sin by using our free will to do so.

God also gave us free will so we can choose him on purpose. The choice for Jesus turns our soul in the direction of God. Our soul goes from being neutral or filled with sin to becoming spiritually "good."

The (human) spirit, that impersonal force God also gave us, is still hanging around. The (human) spirit never becomes part of who we are. But that spirit is our link to God.

To illustrate the point: Let's imagine your soul as a personal computer. You can sit at your desk and use your personal computer. You can type. You can read. You can play games. Your computer is unique. It has a shiny black case and a spiffy silver emblem on the case. It comes with the biggest screen on the market, an apple red mouse, an ergonomically designed keyboard, and flashy colored lights. Your computer is unlike any other computer.

Your computer also comes with software installed by the computer's maker. This software enables you to connect your computer to the Internet. But the software just sits there, not doing anything until it is activated. That inactive software is like your impersonal spirit. When you decide to run that software, you can then connect your computer to the Internet.

Spiritually, when you decide to say "yes" to Jesus, you run your spiritual software. Your soul is activated toward God. Your spirit is connected to the Holy Spirit. Now you can communicate with God in the Heaven-Wide Web because your impersonal spirit (software) has connected your soul (your unique computer) with God's Spirit (the Internet).

Communication is a two-way process. As a Christian, when you pray, you have the Holy Spirit's leading in response to your prayer.[6] Put in spiritual terms, our impersonal spirit (force, ability, pathway) starts out unconnected to God. When we make a choice for Jesus, our soul (who we are as an individual) turns toward good and we receive the Holy Spirit. Our impersonal spirit can then connect and communicate with the Holy Spirit in us. This new connection between our spirit and the Holy Spirit helps us attune ourselves to the leading of the Holy Spirit in us. This communication between the Holy Spirit and our spirit is referred to clearly in Scripture.

> The [Holy] Spirit himself testifies with our spirit that we are God's children (Rom 8:16; explanation added).

We have both a soul and a spirit.

What does the soul/spirit connection have to do with loving God?

We have this ability to communicate with God, because, having chosen to believe in Jesus, our spirit is connected to God's Holy Spirit. Scripture tells us we are to "pray in the Spirit" (Eph 6:18). Scripture tells us that the Holy Spirit guides our prayer and when we don't know how to pray, the Holy Spirit groans with words we cannot understand (Rom 8:26). The Father, however, can understand the Holy Spirit because it is his Spirit groaning. Prayer—communicating with God—is part of loving God. It is communication that builds our love relationship with him.

Once we make that choice for Jesus, our soul—who we are as individuals—can love God in ways that are unique to each of us. Some people express their love for God by singing hymns. Other people love God by dancing, or painting, or teaching, or writing. In our soul is where we worship God with the talents and abilities he has gifted us with and as led by his Holy Spirit now in our lives.

When we love God with all of our soul and deepen our love for him through the communication route he created, we are loving him as the individual, unique person he made us to be.

Remember: We are to love God with everything we are.

---

6. John 14:16–17, 26

Connection Point: What does it mean to you to love God as the individual, unique soul you are? How might you express that love to him?

Third, love God with your mind

Including mind was not arbitrary

This commandment from Jesus on how to love God relates back to Deuteronomy 6:5 where we are told to love God with our heart, soul, and strength. But in all three of the Gospel accounts of this event, Matthew, Mark, and Luke, Jesus included loving God with all our mind. Was Jesus changing things?

In Luke, Jesus turned the question back to the expert in the law, recording that it was the expert in the law who included loving God with your mind.

> On one occasion an expert in the law stood up to test Jesus. "Teacher," he asked, "what must I do to inherit eternal life?"
>
> "What is written in the Law?" he [Jesus] replied. "How do you read it?"
>
> He [the expert in the law] answered, "'Love the Lord your God with all your heart and with all your soul and with all your strength and with all your mind'; and, 'Love your neighbor as yourself.'"
>
> "You have answered correctly," Jesus replied. "Do this and you will live" (Luke 10:25–27; explanation added).

Jesus' did not argue with the expert in the law, saying, "You can't even quote Scripture correctly." Rather, Jesus in effect confirmed that the inclusion of loving God with your mind, was important. We know this because Jesus said, "You have answered correctly."

In Mark, when Jesus responded about loving God with all your heart, soul, mind, and strength, the expert in the law responded,

> "To love him with all your heart, with all your understanding and with all your strength, and to love your neighbor as yourself is more important than all burnt offerings and sacrifices" (Mark 12:33).

While the quotes of who said what vary slightly between the Gospel recordings, the point of all of them is the same: we are to love God with all our heart, soul, mind, and strength.

Understanding happens in the mind

Christianity is the thinking-person's faith. Loving God with your mind was not merely an addition, an afterthought, or a casual inclusion to this commandment. It is in our minds that our knowledge grows. It is in our minds that this knowledge helps us understand things. As we grow in the knowledge and understanding of God's character and his plan, the more we naturally love him. This more scholarly love is different from the rational love we have in our heart. That is a gut-level, logical response to the evidence of God in our lives. Loving God with your mind is about seeking to know him better on purpose.

Most of the book of Deuteronomy which contains the original Scripture Jesus quoted, refers to talking with others about God. It refers to discussing God. It tells us to meditate on Scripture and teach Scripture to others. All of those actions—talking, discussing, meditating, and teaching, are about loving God intellectually.

Throughout his ministry, Jesus emphasized that we must make a decision and choose him consciously. While that decision might be made in our hearts, at a gut, instinctive level, part of coming to that decision involves thinking it through. Jesus understood people's need to think through what he had to say. Ultimately, people had to work out an understanding of what Jesus was teaching in order for them to make a choice to follow him.

Using our mind is about weighing all aspects of an issue. We look at the pros and cons when making a decision. We meditate on a topic. We read Scripture to research God's plan and his character. We pray about issues and ask God to reveal answers. The mind reacts to all we learn about God.

God wants us to love him with our heart and soul. He also wants us to love him intellectually. God gave us minds. He wants us to love him because it is the smart thing to do. He wants us to understand his plan and his character and love him because that plan and he himself are good and deserving of our love.

That does not mean God requires us to read Scripture daily and plow through piles of biblical commentaries to understand him. But God wants to be known. Part of the way we can know him is by learning about him—through experience as well as through study, and then applying that knowledge—while balancing the other ways we are to love him.

> **To illustrate the point:** Pastor Joe was loved by his congregation. He was a wealth of knowledge about the Bible, about the history of the Jewish people, and about God's character. He spent most of his days reading and studying Scripture.
>
> Pastor Joe loved God passionately, eagerly learning how to love God with his mind. Then one day, God gave Pastor Joe a moment of clarity. Loving God wasn't to be just an intellectual pastime. Within a month, Pastor Joe resigned his position at church, sold his home, and was on an airplane to Cambodia to help rescue girls who had been sold into sex trafficking. He had learned enough about God intellectually for the time being. Now he was learning to love God more in his heart (at a gut level) and in his soul (who he was) by how he lived his life.

This illustration points out the need to love God with everything we are—including, but not only—with our mind.

We use our minds to focus on Christ

Jesus does, however, want us to use our minds effectively. When we focus on things of the world—stress, evil, struggles—we have no peace. Humans fret and stew. We worry and spend our lives in turmoil. Paul tells us instead to focus on the character of Christ.

> Finally, brothers and sisters, whatever is true, whatever is noble, whatever is right, whatever is pure, whatever is lovely, whatever is admirable—if anything is excellent or praiseworthy—think about such things (Phil 4:8).

When we focus on the character of Christ—His truth, nobility, righteousness, purity, loveliness, admirable qualities, excellence, and worthiness, and what we have learned about Christ, we will have God's peace. While that peace infers a lack of strife and contentment with things in our life, peace in the New Testament also means something more. Something that relates to loving God with our minds.

For Greater Depth

> Hebrews 12:14 says *Make every effort to live in peace with everyone.* Interestingly, the original Greek word used in this particular verse, *eirene*, affirms that God, the dispenser of peace, expects peace from His people, meaning that he expects the absence of confusion.[7]
>
> Two general definitions of peace are used in the New Testament related to this passage. First, peace involves a tranquil state of a soul assured of its salvation through Christ. The soul fears nothing from God and is therefore content with its earthly lot, whatever that is. Second, peace is a state of conscious reconciliation between ourselves and God.[8]

Definitions of the word *peace* used throughout the New Testament then, include having an absence of confusion, being assured of salvation through Christ, and having a conscious reconciliation with God. Those aspects of peace all have to do with an established, intellectual understanding of God's character and plan. The result of that intellectual process is that we love God with our mind. We will also have the mind of Christ.

> In your relationships with one another, have the same mindset as Christ Jesus (Phil 2:5).

Here is another verse about having the mind of Christ.

> Set your minds on things above, not on earthly things (Col 3:2).

How can the Holy Spirit guide and direct us? Our soul and the Holy Spirit are connected by our spirit (the pathway to communicate with God). Through that connection, the Holy Spirit can remind us (who we are individually; our soul) of what Christ taught, helping us have his mind.

We are also to renew our minds.

> Do not conform to the pattern of this world, but be transformed by the renewing of your mind. Then you will be able to test and

---

7. Zodhiates, *Dictionary*, 519, code 1515(V)
8. Zodhiates, *Dictionary*, 520, code 1515(VII)

approve what God's will is—his good, pleasing and perfect will (Rom 12:2).

We renew our minds by continuously focusing on God. We seek to know God's plan and his character. We focus, meditate, and understand. We then determine how we can best participate in his plan and try to be more like his character. When we understand what we believe and why, our faith is strengthened. Understanding makes our love for God rational, logical, and wise. We can then share our faith and our love for God more easily and more passionately with others.

God gave us minds and wants us to use them. He gave us the ability to sort through information, to weigh knowledge, to understand the things of this world as well as deeper spiritual truths. He created his plan of salvation in a way that requires us to make a conscious decision to accept Jesus as our Savior. When we use our minds to understand God's plan and his character, our natural human response is to love him more.

Remember: We are to love God with everything we are.

Connection Point: The caution to us is that while God wants us to learn about him, he doesn't want us to overthink our faith. We can learn about God with our minds and then set some of the academics aside and focus on the result of the learning: loving God with our mind. Which aspect of loving God with your mind is a new way of looking at it?

Fourth, love God with your strength

The word *strength* conjures up images of Samson, pulling down the palace pillars and of young David defeating the giant with a slingshot and a pocket full of pebbles. There are in fact different types of strength. God wants us to love him with all of our strength and with all types of strength. Let's look at the words used in the New Testament for *strength*.

Love God with All Your Heart, Soul, Mind, and Strength

For Greater Depth

> Mark and Luke use the Greek word *ischus* for *strength*.[9] Paul uses the Greek word *dunamis*.[10] Both of those words refer to endurance, power, and authority and both include physical strength. They also refer to inherent (innate; natural; inborn) power and authority we have within us.

Our internal power and authority are based on who we are and the choices we make. There are also other ways to love God with power, authority, and strength. How do we relate that to loving God?

- Loving God with internal authority is loving God by our free will choice. When we choose God on purpose—at that gut level and then with our souls and minds, we show him our love. That love is based on our internal authority—our decision to love him. Using God's Gift of free will to make a choice to love him is about loving God with internal authority.

- Loving God with his gift of internal strength of will has to do with our grin-and-bear-it strength. I am going to love God through it all—the fear, the uncertainty, the struggle, the pain, the hardship. I. Am. Going. To. Love. God. This internal strength of will is using God's gift of endurance to allow us to love him no matter what is going on in our lives.

- Loving God with our own physical power incorporates the gifts we have received from God. God gave us physical abilities, a life to live. He places us in situations and gives us opportunities. Loving God with our own physical power is about us recognizing those abilities, lives, situations, and opportunities and physically utilizing the gifts God has given us to participate in his plan. Loving God with the physical power he gave us is about making a choice to love God and following through on showing it in the world.

- Loving God with the authority, power, and strength we get from him has to do with accepting authority, power, and strength spiritually received from the Holy Spirit. The Holy Spirit adds to our own power

9. Zodhiates, *Dictionary*, 787–788
10. Zodhiates, *Dictionary*, 485–486

Principle 4 | How Did Jesus Fulfill the Law

and gives us the ability to do more, withstand more, go beyond what we could do on our own.

Need a couple of verses to give you encouragement about the strength we get from God?

> For the Spirit God gave us does not make us timid, but gives us power, love and self-discipline (2 Tim 1:7).

Here is another verse.

> I can do all this through him who gives me strength (Phil 4:13).

Back to Paul's use of the Greek word *dunamis*. One of the themes throughout many of Paul's letters is that of running a race. Paul's race refers to living a life of faith in Christ. It is about walking with Jesus—but not meandering. This is not a speed race, but a long-distance, endurance race. It requires spiritual training in the form of study, meditation, prayer, changing habits, and renewing our minds. It requires strength of character and strength of will. More than anything, it requires the strength we can receive through the Holy Spirit working in us.

To illustrate the point: Let's look at the Apostle Paul's life as an example.

One day Saul headed out gleefully to locate and persecute more of those Jesus people. Then Jesus showed up and blinded him, renaming him Paul, right there on the road to Damascus.

"Saul," Jesus' voice said, "why are you persecuting me?"

Saul (soon renamed Paul by Jesus) was stunned. And overwhelmed. And humbled. Paul was fiercely passionate about God. Wasn't his passion for persecuting Christians a righteous way to honor God? He thought so.

Paul was wrong. But Jesus gave Paul another chance to get it right. Paul was confronted by Christ, converted by Christ, and empowered by the Holy Spirit. The rest of his life, Paul used that fierce passion of his to share the Gospel with the world. Since that day on the dusty road to Damascus, Paul led millions of people to understand the gift Jesus offers to each of us—both during his lifetime and through his letters recorded for us.

That's using Paul's own strength and multiplying it a million billion trillion times with the strength he received from the Holy Spirit at work in him.

We might have strength on our own. That strength, however, can be used either for God or for Satan. Only when we are guided by the Holy Spirit, are we assured that our fierce strength and passion is used to love God. We can love God with our own strength as well as with His.

With that in mind, Paul reminds us that the same power that raised Jesus from the dead is available to us who believe.

> I pray that the eyes of your heart may be enlightened in order that you may know the hope to which he has called you, the riches of his glorious inheritance in his holy people, and his incomparably great power for us who believe. That power is the same as the mighty strength he exerted when he raised Christ from the dead and seated him at his right hand in the heavenly realms (Eph 1:18–20; emphasis added).

In short, we have strength of internal authority to freely choose God, internal strength of will to grin-and-bear-it, and physical strength to work hard to do what is pleasing to God. And God surely loves that we love him with those types of strength. But God also gave us the Holy Spirit—a full serving of his divine power in our lives. Thus in addition to our own personal strength of authority, strength of will, and strength of endurance, we also have available to us the same power that raised Jesus from the dead. We have the authority, power, and strength of God.

Because we have God's strength, everything we do—including loving God—is stronger. We have the power of God in us—to love him in a way that is stronger than we could love him if we didn't have that power. We are to love God with all our (and his) strength. That's a whole lot of love.

Some of us express our love for God in an emotional manner. No doubt, God accepts emotional love, too. However, it is emotions that become a spiritual battlefield for many people. It is emotionally that we are most easily impacted by the world around us. By loving God with all of our heart, soul, mind, and strength, we are more solidly focused and spiritually protected, thus being able to better resist emotional attack by the world. Emotions may be fleeting. Emotions may be unstable. Emotions may have highs and lows depending on what else is going on in the world around us.

But we can be grounded in our hearts, in our souls, in our minds, and with our own and God's strength. That spiritual grounding allows us to endure more when tempted and be less likely to be affected by outside influences. This commandment to love God in all these ways is a benefit for our faith. It is a way to be more steadfast in what we believe and in our relationship with God.

Remember: We are to love God with everything we are.

> **Connection Point**: What does loving God with your strength mean to you? How might you love God better with your own strength multiplied by the power of God in you?

Chapter Summary

- **Theology Simplified:** When we make a decision in our heart for Jesus, our soul is directed toward God. That enables us to love God with our hearts and with our Holy Spirit-connected souls. We use our minds to understand what we believe, loving God more as we understand more about his plan and character. We can also love God utilizing our own strength as well as relying on his power. The heart, soul, mind, and strength are the ways Jesus reminded us that we are to love God. They are *where* or *with what* within us that we can love him. Loving God with our heart, soul, mind, and strength, means loving him with everything we are and in every way we can.

- **What's it to me?** There's a lot to that first and greatest commandment Jesus quoted. But God has provided many ways to help you love him more. God doesn't *need y*our love. But he wants your love, because he knows that the more you love him, the closer your relationship with him becomes. The closer your relationship with him, the more he can express his love to you. And the more you are blessed.

- **Faith Simplified:** God wants us to love him with everything we are.

13

How Do I Love Others as Myself?

IN THE LAST CHAPTER, we talked about the ways we can love God. We might also refer to them as *where* within us we are to love God. We are to love God *with* (or in, or using) our heart, soul, mind, and strength—with every part of us and with everything we are.

The second commandment Jesus shared was to love your neighbor as yourself. But when we think about putting that simple commandment into practice, we have questions. What kind of love is Jesus talking about? How do I love my neighbor when I don't even like him? What does it mean to love myself? How can I love others in that way?

As we focus on the answers to these questions, let's remember that the most important, underlying aspect of this commandment is simple: Love others.

The four types of biblical love

Nowhere does Scripture say we have to like anyone. Or agree with anyone. Or hang out with anyone. It is only our modern definition of love that makes us think we should do those things. As often happens, we define ancient words based on our modern understanding. So what exactly did Jesus mean when he talked about love? There are four Greek words for love: *agape, phileo, storge,* and *eros* love. Which kind of love did Jesus mean?

Principle 4 | How Did Jesus Fulfill the Law

Agape love is unconditional love by commitment

For Greater Depth

> The Greek word most often used in the New Testament, relating to love for others is *agape*. While the definition includes duty, commitment, and goodwill, the underlying definition for *agape* love includes the need to not necessarily do what pleases others, but to provide what they need.[1]

Agape love is the kind of love God the Father has for mankind. God is committed to loving us and doing so unconditionally. God may not like what we do at times, but he still loves us. God's *agape* love is seen in Scripture through God's covenants to individuals and to mankind.

Agape love is about providing what a person needs; not necessarily what they want or think they want. Sometimes we ask God for what we think we "need," but then he answers our prayers by providing us with what is better; what we actually need, not necessarily what we had wanted. The Old Testament Jewish people wanted a Messiah who would be a powerful, political king to save them from oppressive rulers. Instead, God sent Jesus—a powerful, eternal king to save them from the oppressive dark ruler who wants our souls. That exemplifies God's *agape* love for us. He gave us what we needed. In all three Gospel accounts, the word for love Jesus used in the commandment to love God was *agape* love.

Jesus also used the word, *agape* in the three gospels when he commanded us to love other people. *Agape* love for other people is directed by will. To love others with *agape* love requires a conscious effort to love them and a commitment to do so. Although there is a sense of underlying goodwill and benevolence, *agape* love in action, might include discipline or even punishment, just as God the Father's *agape* love for us might.

> the LORD disciplines those he loves, as a father the son he delights in (Prov 3:12).

To illustrate the point: Our *agape* love toward other people would involve doing or giving people what they need, rather than what they want. If a person asks for money because they

---

1. Zodhiates, *Dictionary*, 66–67

continue to spend unwisely, an example of *agape* love would be to teach them about money management instead of handing them cash. If a country which was our enemy asked for military help amid a civil war, an example of *agape* love would be to send food or medicine instead. The opposite of *agape* love would be neglect, disregard, or condemnation.

God does not require us to befriend our enemies.

> don't you know that friendship with the world means enmity against God? Therefore, anyone who chooses to be a friend of the world becomes an enemy of God.[2]

We are told never to adopt the interests of our enemies—being those who do not know Christ. Rather, we are to love them with *agape* love. We are to do whatever is needed to turn them to Christ—in their best interests; not necessarily what they want, but what they need. What they need most is Jesus.

Connection Point: Have you ever asked God for what you thought you needed only to have him reveal to you what you *really* need? What did you learn from that experience about the way he loves you?

Phileo love is love for friends

For Greater Depth

> The Greek word *philos* refers to love between friends or brotherly love. With brotherly love, there are often common interests between friends and joy in being together.[3]

The term *philos* is almost never used to refer to God the Father's love toward us or our love for him. We cannot declare ourselves to be friends with God the Father, as our relationship with him cannot be as equals. Only God can declare us his friend, as he did with Abraham.

---

2. Jas 4:4; see also Eph 2:2; John 3:36
3. Zodhiates, *Dictionary*, 1447

And the scripture was fulfilled that says, "Abraham believed God, and it was credited to him as righteousness," and he was called God's friend (Jas 2:23 referring to Isa 41:8).

Once more for emphasis: God the Father can declare us his friend, but we cannot declare God the Father our friend. That verse from Isaiah is the only time in the Old Testament when a person was referred to as being "a friend of God."[4] Jesus, however, did call his disciples *philos* friends, indicating his warm personal affection for them.

> "I no longer call you servants, because a servant does not know his master's business. Instead, I have called you friends, for everything that I learned from my Father I have made known to you" (John 15:15).

As Jesus has also told us modern disciples everything that has been recorded in Scripture, we too can be called his friend. But notice that Jesus is the one who declared us his friend first; not the other way around.

As it relates to other Christians, we might ultimately have brotherly *philos* love for them also. But *philos* love is not the kind of love Jesus said to have for people who do not know him. *Agape* love is for them.

Connection Point: Is there a person in your church community you have a brotherly love for? Is there someone who is not a Christian who you thought you had brotherly love for? How might you reach out to that person with *agape* love?

Storge love is love for family

For Greater Depth

> The Greek word used to express love of family is *storge*. *Storge* love involves a sense of affiliation among people. The specific word *storge* is referred to with examples of Mary and Marth's love for their brother, Lazarus as well as people's relationship within the new church, where the word *phileostorgos* is used to indicate both friendship and a sense of family.[5]

---

4. Although Exod 33:11 says God spoke to Moses "as one who speaks to a friend," it does not say God actually declared Moses a friend, only that he spoke to Moses that way.

5. Zodhiates, *Dictionary,* 1448

We love our parents and our siblings differently than we love our friends and our spouse. *Storge* is often combined in the New Testament with *phileo* love and termed *philostorgos*. *Philostorgos* love was exemplified in the early Church. The relationship among other believers back then included both friendship as well as a sense of affiliation. It also included the understanding that all Christians are one big family, having been adopted by God.

> **Connection Point**: Who in your life do you have *storge* love for? Are there people who are not your family biologically for whom you have *storge* love? How is *storge* love different from love for your non-Christian family members?

The fourth type of Greek love is *eros* love. *Eros* love is romantic love exemplified by love between spouses. Obviously, *eros* love is not the type of love we are to have for our neighbors.

Basically, biblically, we can love others with *agape* love, or *phileo*, *storge*, or *phileostorgos* love, depending on our relationship with them. Those are the types of love we are to have. In Jesus' commandment, however, the type of love he was referring to for us to love others was *agape* love. We are to unconditionally love other people, by commitment and by will, providing what they need.

Who is our neighbor?

When the expert in the law asked Jesus this question in Luke, Jesus followed the commandment with the parable of the Good Samaritan. The Jews and Samaritans were hostile toward each other at the time of that parable. It was the hated Samaritan in the story, however, who helped the Jewish man in need. The expert in the law, recognized the Samaritan—the person who had shown mercy—as the true neighbor of the man in need.

Showing mercy to everyone thus makes us a neighbor to everyone. We are to love them, leaving justice to God to render. Applying this definition to Jesus' parable, we are to have *agape* love for others, whether they know Jesus or not.

For Greater Depth

> The specific word used in Luke 10:37 for *mercy* is the Greek word *eleos*. *Eleos* means to have compassion, especially compassion or mercy on a person in unhappy circumstances. *Eleos* involves an active desire to remove those miseries.[6]

Jesus then tells us specifically that we are to love people *everywhere*.

> "But you will receive power when the Holy Spirit comes upon you. And you will be my witnesses, telling people about me everywhere—in Jerusalem, throughout Judea, in Samaria, and to the ends of the earth" (Acts 1:8).

Jesus was speaking to his disciples. As modern disciples, Jesus was also speaking to us. Perhaps we cannot go to Jerusalem, to the area that was once Judea and Samaria, or to the ends of the earth. But we certainly can tell people about Jesus everywhere we are. In short, everyone, everywhere is our neighbor.

Connection Point: Is there someone in your life who you do not consider your neighbor but who you should? How might you love that person as the Samaritan did?

How do we love others as ourselves?

Some people struggle with the idea of loving themselves. We may feel shame or remorse for our past. We may feel inferior or insignificant when we compare ourselves to others. We may not feel we can love ourselves emotionally or even like ourselves. Before we feel capable of loving others then, we may have to learn to first love ourselves in two ways.

First, we can love ourselves as one of God's creations. At each step of Creation, God saw that what he had created "was good." God loves all of his creations, but he especially loves us people. Finally, after God created man and woman, God declared it "very good." He created us—all of us—as "very good."

---

6. Zodhiates, *Dictionary*, 564–565

To illustrate the point: God especially loves those of us who believe in his Son, Jesus. He loves us as his dearly-loved child. Jesus loves us as a person he gave his life for. The Holy Spirit loves us as the temple he inhabits. All three persons of the Trinity find us worthy of their unconditional love. Who are we to argue with God?

Second, we can love ourselves by duty, taking care of ourselves because it is our responsibility. The very first thing God entrusted us with was our bodies. We are to feed them nutritious food. We are to drink cleansing water. We are to move our muscles and strengthen them. We are to do whatever we need to do to keep them healthy. Doing what we need to do for our own benefit (whether physically or spiritually) is an example of *agape* love for ourselves. Jesus wants us to love others in that same way.

We don't always want to eat healthy food. We don't always want to exercise. But when we love ourselves, we know that the best, most loving thing we can do for our bodies is to take care of them in the way they need to be taken care of.

Spiritually, some days we don't feel like reading our Bible. Some days we don't feel like thanking God for our food. But we know that maintaining our relationship with our Heavenly Father is what is best for us. So we read and we pray.

We are to love like Christ did

We are not to define ourselves by what the world says. We are to define ourselves by what Jesus says. So how are we to love ourselves? We have value to God. We are to make sure our needs are met—especially our need for a Savior.

Extending that love to others means recognizing that all people have value to God. They have needs. Like us, their greatest need is for a Savior. We are to help them know Jesus so they can say "yes" to him and make sure their greatest need—salvation—is met.

Before we knew Jesus, we were God's enemy.[7] But the Father nevertheless loved us with *agape* love. He was nevertheless committed to loving us unconditionally. He nevertheless supplied what we needed. Even before we were born, he provided a plan of salvation for us through Jesus.

---

7. See Jas 4:4; Rom 5:10

When we learn to love ourselves the way God loves us—unconditionally, with duty and responsibility, and by commitment—we can extend that *agape* love toward others. We can love our neighbors and even our enemies the way God loved us before we became his children.

It is not our duty to like non-believers individually or even know them personally. We are simply to love others as ourselves, not embracing their interests but doing what is necessary for them to make it easy for them to accept the grace offered by Jesus.

Jesus told us to go into the world and make disciples of others who do not already know him.

> Therefore go and make disciples of all nations, baptizing them in the name of the Father and of the Son and of the Holy Spirit, and teaching them to obey everything I have commanded you. And surely I am with you always, to the very end of the age" (Matt 28:19–20).

A disciple of Jesus is a student or follower, who listens to the teachings of Jesus, ready to make a choice for him. Jesus never told us to make people believers or to save anyone. Only Jesus can do that. Rather, we are to teach people about Jesus, so they can make the logical choice for him as he is working on their hearts.

For Greater Depth

> The original Greek word used for *go make disciples* is *matheteuo*.[8] The International Standard Version of this verse says, "as you go, disciple people." The King James Version says, "teach all nations." Jesus did not tell his disciples to go out and save people. Jesus is the only one who saves. All his disciples can do—including us—is teach about him.
>
> Those versions are helpful in understanding the meaning of *disciple*. We cannot save people or turn them into believers. All we are commissioned by Jesus to do is teach others about him and let him take it from there.

---

8. Zodhiates, *Dictionary*, 935

Telling people about Jesus is the most important way God wants us to love others with *agape* love. We are to love others by providing what they need most—hearing about Jesus, even if it is not politically correct or culturally acceptable. People's need for Jesus is more important than cultural norms.

> **Connection Point**: Are you a disciple or a believer of Jesus? Do you know someone who is still learning about Jesus but has not yet made the commitment to become a believer? How might you encourage that person to take the next step?

Apply the "where" (heart, soul, mind, strength) to the "how" (biblical love)

Let's return to those two greatest commandments. After loving God, Jesus said that the second commandment (loving others) is like the first.

> Jesus replied: "'Love the Lord your God with all your heart and with all your soul and with all your mind.' This is the first and greatest commandment. And the second is like it: 'Love your neighbor as yourself.'" (Matt 22:37–39; emphasis added).

If the second commandment is like the first, it is implied that we should love others with the same abilities (mechanism or where—the heart, soul, mind, and strength) that we love God the Father.

- We can love others with our hearts, making a gut-level decision, to do so—in our inmost being. We can recognize our duty to love nonbelievers by sharing the Gospel with them and praying for them. We can recognize our responsibility to love other Christians by encouraging them, working alongside them, praying for them, and being unified with them.

- We can love others with our soul by recognizing good and evil, standing up against evil, not embracing evil, but *agape*-ly loving people who do embrace evil. We can employ our individuality and the gifts and abilities God has given us to share Jesus with others and encourage other believers. We can live a life like Christ and be an example to others.

- We can love others with our minds, to see people at an intellectual level, rather than an emotional one. We can understand what they need, whether it is the Gospel, food or other assistance (See Jas 2:15–16). We can help them weigh the evidence for Jesus and help them make a decision for him. We can understand our faith and be able to communicate that understanding to others as well as to help other Christians understand and live out their faith, following Peter's advice.

> Aways be prepared to give an answer to everyone who asks you to give the reason for the hope that you have (1 Pet 3:15).

- We can love others with our strength, passionately sharing the Gospel. We can be bold and enthusiastic about sharing what knowing Jesus has meant for us. We can work to build up Christ's church and encourage other believers. We can rely on the Holy Spirit for strength, endurance, and direction.

We don't have to like other people; just love them, starting at a gut, instinctive level. Jesus died for them just as he died for you and me. If they are valuable to him, then we—having the mind of Christ—must value them also.

Chapter Summary

- **Theology Simplified:** We are to be everyone's mercy-showing neighbor. We are to love every person who does not know Jesus with *agape* love until they become *storgos* (family) and *phileostorgos* (friend/family) members of God's family with us. Before people believe, as well as after, we are to love them with our hearts, our souls, our minds, and our strength.
- **What's it to me?** It's hard to love people you don't like. But good news! You don't have to like them. It's hard to love your enemies. But, hey, you were God's enemy before you knew him and he still loved you. It's hard to love people in general. People can be so annoying. But good news, you can start by just committing to love them with *agape* love, knowing Jesus values them, just as much as he values you.
- **Faith Simplified:** God wants us to love others with everything we are, too.

This is the fourth principle of *Faith Simplified*: Love God and love others.

Principle 5

How Are Judgment and Free Will Dangerous Gifts?

14

The Gift of Judgment

He will judge the world in righteousness and the peoples in his faithfulness (Ps 96:13).

Eternal judgment

GOD'S FINAL JUDGMENT WILL determine whether our souls will have eternal life with him—or not. How we react to what Jesus did, is the only thing which affects that determination. Did we say "yes" to Jesus or not? Jesus reminded us,

> "Not everyone who says to me, 'Lord, Lord,' will enter the kingdom of heaven, but only the one who does the will of my Father who is in heaven. Many will say to me on that day, 'Lord, Lord, did we not prophesy in your name and in your name drive out demons and in your name perform many miracles?' Then I will tell them plainly, 'I never knew you. Away from me, you evildoers!' " (Matt 7:21–23)

Some Christians' faith waivers after reading this verse. "I do believe in Jesus," they say quietly. But there is still a doubt about whether their lives will show evidence of that belief. Maybe they think they have not done enough good deeds in life to justify eternity with God. Fortunately, while God surely wants our lives to reflect our faith by doing good deeds, Scripture assures us that it is our heart which God is eternally interested in, not our works.

Or maybe those same Christians think they have not done the "will of the Father." The most important will the Father has for us is to live in Heaven with him. Those Christians have already done the will of the Father when they said "yes" to Jesus. What then is it that God looks at, if it isn't what we did in life?

> The LORD does not look at the things people look at. People look at the outward appearance, but the LORD looks at the heart (1 Sam 16:7).

Why would God look at our hearts (our inmost being)? Because our hearts provide the evidence of our salvation.

The Holy Spirit in our hearts

When we surrender our lives to Jesus, the Holy Spirit takes residence in our hearts. It is because God, the Holy Spirit, lives in our hearts, that God the Father and God, the Son Jesus can judge our hearts without ambiguity.

God looks at our hearts and sees the Holy Spirit residing there. "There I am," the Father says. "I sealed you for this day." So when a person stands before the throne in judgment, there is no question about salvation. The Holy Spirit is either in your heart or not. If not, Jesus will say, "I never knew you." He doesn't look at how many good deeds you did or did not do in life. He looks at your heart because it is your heart that holds the evidence—the presence of the Holy Spirit.

But how can I trust that the Holy Spirit will still be with me when I die? Because God promised to be with us always. The way God can do that is through the Holy Spirit in us. Here's what Jesus promised:

> "And I will ask the Father, and he will give you another advocate to help you and be with you forever—the Spirit of truth" (John 14:16–17; emphasis added).

Did you see that? The Spirit will be with you forever. Forever includes that moment when we stand before the throne. Need more verses that God promises not to leave us? Here is a good one:

> "And surely I am with you *always*, to the very end of the age."[1]

---

1. Matt 28:20; emphasis added; see also Deut 31:6 quoted in Heb 13:5; Ps 94:14

The Gift of Judgment

When we receive Jesus' gift of the Holy Spirit, our forgiven hearts are sealed, so that they now and forever belong to God. God claimed ownership of us for the day of judgment. We belong to him. It's guaranteed because his Spirit—God himself—is right there in our hearts, saying so.

> Now it is God who makes both us and you stand firm in Christ. He anointed us, set his seal of ownership on us, and put his Spirit in our hearts as a deposit, guaranteeing what is to come (2 Cor 1:21–22).

Here's another verse about the sealing by the Holy Spirit.

> And do not grieve the Holy Spirit of God, with whom you were sealed for the day of redemption (Eph 4:30).[2]

For Greater Depth

> The original Greek word used in Ephesians 4:30 for *sealed* is *sphragizo* which means: to set a seal or mark upon a thing as a token of its authenticity or approvedness.[3] The Holy Spirit is God's pledge or seal of our election to salvation.

Once sealed, we are then sanctified. "Stop using big words!" you say. Sanctification just means we have been set apart for God (and by God) as one element of that sealing. Think of it as God picking his baseball team. "I call dibs on you," he says pointing right at you. You are set apart for God. On his team. Forever. Guaranteed.

It is the Holy Spirit who does the sanctification. It is the Holy Spirit who seals us. It is the Holy Spirit who guarantees our salvation through Jesus. Once more, God is not only guaranteeing his part of the New Covenant, he is guaranteeing our part too, by completing our part of that covenant himself.

After the Holy Spirit dwells in us, the Holy Spirit then begins a process of purification. We have already been made holy and sanctified from the point of view that we now belong to God. The ongoing process of becoming

---

2. See additional verses about the Holy Spirit being an active participant: John 14:16-17; 15:26; 16:33; Rom 5:5; 8:26-27; 1 Corin 2:11; 3:16; Gal 4:6
3. Zodhiates, *Dictionary,* 1351–1352

(further) holy, implies a new and continuing process which is done—not by us—but by the Holy Spirit.

What was that again? The process of becoming further holy is done by the Holy Spirit; not by us.

> In all my prayers for all of you, I always pray with joy because of your partnership in the gospel from the first day until now, being confident of this, that he who began a good work in you will carry it on to completion until the day of Christ Jesus (Phil 1:4–6; emphasis added).

God began a good work when you said "yes" to Jesus. From that moment on, he will keep working in us. The good work God is doing is an action that will be finished only on the day of Jesus' return. We are encouraged to listen to the guidance of the Holy Spirit. We are encouraged to follow the Spirit's guidance. It is the Spirit though, not us, doing the work. We are not working to earn salvation.

The Holy Spirit works in us. The Holy Spirit keeps working in us. The Holy Spirit is also the evidence of our surrender to Jesus. God the Father is able to judge our hearts because that is where his holy presence resides. On judgment day, we stand before the throne and—bam!—all those spiritual charts and color-coded graphs we toiled over; all those detailed records of what great things we did in life are useless. The Father doesn't need them. He has an expert witness. God's Spirit dwelling right there in our heart is first-person testimony that our heart belongs to him.

For Greater Depth

> In the following verses from the book of Hebrews, the original Greek word *hagiazo* was used to refer to this ongoing process—being sanctified by the Holy Spirit. The use of *hagiazo* in those phrases—those who are being made holy; and the one who makes (and continues to make) people holy—describe an action that is unfinished.[4]
>
> For by one sacrifice he has made perfect forever *those who are being made holy* (Heb 10:14, emphasis added).
>
> And,

---

4. Zodhiates, *Dictionary*, 69–70

The Gift of Judgment

> Both *the one who* makes people holy and those who are made holy are of the same family. So Jesus is not ashamed to call them brothers and sisters (Heb 2:11; emphasis added).

Connection Point: How do you feel knowing that, if you have said "yes" to Jesus, the presence of the Holy Spirit in you is undeniable proof of your salvation to all three persons of the Trinity? Does that explanation help you better understand Matthew 2:21–23 and why Jesus would not know a person if the Holy Spirit wasn't in his heart, no matter what good deeds he had done in life?

To illustrate the point: George accepts the salvation and forgiveness given by Jesus. The Holy Spirit resides in George and guides his life. He does some things right; he does some things not quite right. He does some things quite wrong. But George continues to claim Jesus as his Savior and continues to try to live a life worthy of Jesus. Then George dies and stands before the Great White Throne.

God the Father, sitting on the throne, is ready to judge George. The Holy Spirit explains the condition of George's heart and shows the Father the seal the Holy Spirit has placed spiritually on George's heart as evidence of George's salvation. Both the Holy Spirit and Jesus claim George's heart. George's heart is therefore judged right with God. All three persons of the Trinity are in agreement.

Evelyn, on the other hand, has not surrendered her life to Jesus. She volunteered at a shelter each week, serving lunch to the homeness. She chaired the committee of her women's club to raise thousands of dollars each year for various charities that benefitted children. She regularly made dinners for her elderly neighbor.

Despite all the kind things she did for others, when Evelyn stands before the throne, Jesus will tell the Father that he does not know her. The Father will look into her heart and see that the Holy Spirit does not live there. There is no seal on her heart evidencing her surrender to Jesus. Therefore, based on a judgment of the heart, Evelyn will not inherit the kingdom of God. Her soul will not live eternally in Heaven.

No matter how "good" of a life a nonbeliever has lived; no matter how much money a nonbeliever has given to charities; no matter how many hours a nonbeliever has toiled for betterment of other people, the environment, or human rights—without Jesus, that person never gets beyond the judgment of the heart. Without Jesus, all of those dollars and hours of work are never judged worthy. The Holy Spirit is not living in that heart. There is no seal. The Holy Spirit is not present.

> For God so loved the world that he gave his one and only Son, that whoever believes in him shall not perish but have eternal life (John 3:16).

Here's what Scripture tells us:

- All people will be judged
- God will do the judging
- God's judgment determines what happens to a person's eternal soul (the individual person he is)
- God created the process of salvation only through Christ
- God judges by looking at the person's heart
- Evidence of whether a person belongs to Christ is the presence of the Holy Spirit in their heart

The gift part of judgment

One of the greatest gifts God has given us is the gift to *not judge*. We do not have the authority, the responsibility, the power, duty, or the ability to judge other people's hearts. Not having to judge others relieves us of an enormous burden. We can simply leave judgment up to God to take care of.

Whew! Thank you, God for not making us responsible for keeping the earth spinning. Thank you, God for not having us make sure the stars don't fall out of the sky. Thank you, God for relieving us of the duty to judge the hearts of other people!

The Gift of Judgment

> Do not judge, and you will not be judged. Do not condemn, and you will not be condemned. Forgive, and you will be forgiven (Luke 6:37).

Only God can see a person's heart. Only God can decide where a person spends eternity. We are not to try to be like God or take on any of his responsibilities. Even if we attempted to judge a person's heart properly, we couldn't see whether the Holy Spirit was present. And since God has the final say, what we think is irrelevant anyway.

Although God has relieved us of the duty to judge other people's hearts, we sometimes declare someone bad or not Christian. We judge without being able to see inside their hearts. We judge instead of forgiving. God may have future plans for that person that will change the status of their hearts. We can leave it all to God and move on to pay attention to the Holy Spirit inside *us*.

That tendency of us to want to judge others is the dangerous part of judgment. It's not God's judgment of us we should worry about. We're sealed forever, remember? Rather the danger is us trying to judge the hearts or the faith of others. That's like us trying to take on some of God's job. Eve wanted to be like God, too. Her desire led her to that big sin with big consequences.

Sometimes, Christians *do* judge others. We say, "That's not a biblical way to live." "Scripture says that's a sin." Are we hypocrites if we judge people in this way? Other Scripture tells us we have a responsibility to correct the thoughts and actions of people in our lives. Isn't that a form of judging? Or is it something different? Let's look at that next.

> **Connection Point**: It is hard not to judge other people—their motives, their actions, and their faith. How does it make you feel that God is the only one who can judge? Does it relieve you to know you are not to judge other people in that way?

Chapter Summary

- **Theology Simplified:** When we surrender to Jesus, the Holy Spirit takes up residence in our hearts, declaring us holy (belonging to God) and sanctified (set apart for God's purpose). The Spirit seals our hearts eternally, providing evidence of our faith. God has gifted us by relieving us of the burden of judging others.

- **What's it to me?** If your spirit is connected to God because of Jesus, your soul will live eternally in Heaven. The Holy Spirit has placed an unbreakable seal on your heart. Even if you don't always do what God might have in mind for you to do, your salvation is still guaranteed because you said "yes" to Jesus. And all those people you think are weird or bad or not good Christians? You can leave judgment of their hearts in God's hands. He knows what to do.
- **Faith Simplified:** God will judge people's hearts based on whether the Holy Spirit dwells in it. We don't judge anyone.

15

Discernment

Discernment is not knowing the difference between right and wrong. It is knowing the difference between right and almost right.[1]

What is discernment?

KNOWING RIGHT FROM WRONG and good from evil is an inherent gift we received as a result of Eve's disobedience. Combined with information we gain through study and experience, we can obtain wisdom in general. But we also need discernment that comes from knowing what the Bible says, understanding what it means, and applying it correctly.

God will take care of judging the hearts of people. Not having the duty to judge others takes an enormous burden from us. It is one of God's greatest gifts to us. That leaves us to exercise discernment.

> And this is my prayer: that your love may abound more and more in knowledge and depth of insight, so that you may be able to discern what is best and may be pure and blameless for the day of Christ, (Phil 1:9–10; emphasis added).

Biblical discernment is a process of testing everything against what we know about God's plan and his character through our understanding of

---

1. Theologian C. H. Spurgeon is typically credited for this statement

Scripture and our relationship with him. Discernment has a more specific focus than knowledge of good and evil or wisdom in general. Discernment has to do with seeing the difference between right and wrong, and truth from lies, or recognizing false thinking in individual instances. It is an ability to distinguish between things; an ability to examine and test things and compare them to God's standard. We might look at the process of gaining discernment like this:

- We start with God-given *knowledge of good and evil*. Then . . .
- We ask God for *wisdom* in how to use that knowledge. Then . . .
- We gain *experience* and *understanding* in our daily lives and through learning about God's character and his plan

All these enable us to examine and test things (discern them) in specific instances.

How do we apply discernment?

For Greater Depth

> The *King James Dictionary* defines *discernment* as examination, testing, scrutinization.[2] Notice the definition does not include judging with a final determination.

The knowledge of good and evil gives humanity the ability to know what is good and what is evil. That knowledge includes actions that are good or evil or actions that result in good or evil. It is those actions we are to judge. The judging of actions is a form of discernment. But discernment should never lead to judgment of the heart; only to judge actions so as to protect ourselves and others.

The difference between discernment (or judging an action) and judging a person's heart, may not sound like a big deal. But it is a very big deal to God. When we judge a person's heart, we are attempting to know where they stand in their relationship with God. We are attempting to know their value in God's eyes. We are attempting to put ourselves on equal footing with God himself.

2. *King James Dictionary*, s.v. "discern (v.)"

Bad idea. Every time.

Let's look at examples of how we might discern a person's actions without judging their heart.

Discernment Example 1

A person has lied to us many times. We forgive that person. For our own protection or the protection of others, however, we should not trust what they say without examination, because that could lead to injustice for us or for other people. Not trusting what they say because of their past actions is discernment.

Discernment for our future protection is our part of the process; forgiveness is our part of the process. Our part of the process is also to leave judgment of that person's heart up to God. From our perspective, our mental process would be:

- *Knowledge*: lying is evil (1 Pet 3:10)
- God's *wisdom* and our *experience*: lying is injustice and hurts people
- Application of *discernment*: we are not required to trust a person who has lied, even if we have forgiven the person and left judgment of their heart to God.

Discernment about actions involves protection of ourselves and others.

Discernment Example 2

We meet someone with a new theology. Maybe the person declares we should worship the god within each of us. The person might sound eloquent; might even be persuasive; might phrase the argument in a way that sounds biblical, referencing perhaps the Holy Spirit in us but confusing a worship of the Holy Spirit with a worship of our spirit. In such an instance, we need to be able to discern what is not quite right.

We still cannot judge the heart of the person. We can, however, use biblical discernment about what they say to protect our spiritual health and well-being and that of others. And we can attempt to help the person correct their theology.

From our perspective, our mental process would be:

- *Knowledge*: theological thinking that is not biblical is evil (Col 2:8)
- God's *wisdom* and our *experience*: unbiblical theology can lead us astray
- Application of *discernment*: we are not to believe a person with false teaching, even if we have left judgment of their heart to God.

Discernment about actions involves protection of ourselves and others.

Discernment Example 3

We might know a person who has been judicially judged a child molester. Perhaps the person has been punished. Perhaps the person has even repented and said he had been forgiven by Christ. We, however, do not know the person's heart. We can hope the person has repented and hope he will never molest a child again. But discernment tells us that an application of wisdom and knowledge means we should not entrust our child to be in that person's presence alone.

From our perspective, our mental process would be:

- *Knowledge*: mistreatment of children is evil (Mark 10:14; Matt 18:6)
- God's *wisdom* and our *experience*: we must protect children from evil
- Application of *discernment*: we must protect our children from potential evil, even if we have left judgment of a person's heart to God.

Discernment about actions involves protection of ourselves and others.

We are specifically told not to judge unbelievers

> What business is it of mine to *judge those outside the church*? Are you not to judge those inside? God will judge those outside (1 Cor 5:12–13; emphasis added).

Unbelievers are not exempt from judgment. But we are not to do the judging. We are to discern their actions and protect ourselves and others as needed. The challenge is not to extend the discernment of actions to judging their hearts. We are to leave eternal judgment about the status of their hearts to God. We can only introduce them to Jesus and let Jesus work on their hearts.

Connection Point: Have you ever struggled with the difference between judgment and discernment of other people? What can you do to remember the differences and follow God's leading on this?

Judgment of other believers

Let's look again at what Paul said to the Corinthians.

> What business is it of mine to judge those outside the church? Are you not to judge those inside? God will judge those outside.

Paul told the Corinthians that God will judge people outside the church. We are to judge those inside. Wait. Didn't we just say God gifted us by not having the authority, the responsibility, the power, the duty, or the ability to judge others? What does Paul mean by judging other believers?

For Greater Depth

> The use of the word *krino* in 1 Corinthians 5:12–13, about God judging people outside the church, refers to judging based on those secret things of the heart and specifically on people's acceptance of Jesus.
>
> The use of *krino* about judging those inside the church, however, is defined as judging in the judicial sense after separating and considering the particulars of a case.[3] Note the similarity to the earlier definition of discernment: examination, testing, scrutinization.

---

3. Zodhiates, *Dictionary*, 888–889

Accountability

The judging of people inside the church that Paul was talking about in 1 Corinthians was discerning the actions of believers and lovingly correcting them when their actions do not correspond with Scripture. It is about keeping ourselves and other believers accountable to live what we believe. We believers love Christ and want to live as directed by the Holy Spirit. Sometimes, however, we fail. Paul shared his struggle:

> I do not understand what I do. For what I want to do I do not do, but what I hate I do (Rom 7:15).

We say we follow Jesus. But sometimes our actions do not conform to what Jesus taught. We see our own slip-ups as part of our process of growing in our faith, with God's grace covering us as we stumble. The world, however, looking at us without the lens of Christ's grace, merely sees actions that are not what we profess to believe.

It is the duty of other believers then to look at our actions from the point of our beliefs and call us out on actions that do not coincide with what Jesus tells us to do. We believers still do not have the authority, the responsibility, the power, the duty, or the ability to judge the hearts of other believers, but we do have the responsibility to judge their actions as they relate to what Jesus taught.

The stickler with this discernment is that other believers have the same responsibility to judge our actions and to remind us when we are not living according to what Jesus taught.

> "Why do you look at the speck of sawdust in your brother's eye and pay no attention to the plank in your own eye?" (Matt 7:3)

We have a duty to lovingly address issues in other Christians' lives when their actions do not align with Scripture. We are to question those actions. We are to keep people accountable. And we are to help them stay on the right track. They are to do the same with us.

Through it all, however, we are to remember that the point is to encourage each other. It is about accountability of each other. Judgment tears other people down. By encouraging people to live their beliefs, accountability lifts people up.

We are not to judge another believer's faith or doctrine unrelated to salvation

Over 2,000 years after Christ's death and resurrection, his church has blossomed. While that is a good thing, time has also given rise to many "varieties" of Christianity. The basic doctrines of mainstream Christian denominations are the same as they were 2,000 years ago—belief in God the Father, the Son, and the Holy Spirit. Jesus born of the virgin, Mary. Jesus lived an earthly, sinless life, was crucified to provide a blood sacrifice to forgive our sins. Jesus died, was buried, and was resurrected on the third day, and now is in Heaven, waiting for us believers to spend eternity there with him, the Father, and the Holy Spirit.

Those are the basic principles of Christianity. The single requirement for salvation, set out in Scripture is simple and does not change: Believe in Jesus as Savior.[4] Once saved by that simple belief, we are encouraged to show the world evidence of our salvation—through voicing our faith and sharing the Gospel. But even doing those things are not requirements for salvation. They are actions we take. They are works we do. Did you get that? They are not requirements for salvation.

There are other aspects of Christianity, however, that people focus on (and sometimes fight about) beyond the required simple belief in Jesus as Savior. Groups of people argue about those other focuses. Entire denominations have been established over single actions the founders feel are important enough to separate themselves from other Christian groups. They formalize these aspects into denominational doctrine or disciplines for their members to follow. Whether or not we (or they themselves) follow those doctrines though is not related to salvation.

In Christianity, all that is required for salvation is a belief in Jesus. Scripture clearly says that nothing else we might think is important from our human point of view is required. Anything else might be nice and even godly, but it is not necessary for our soul's eternal life in Heaven.

To illustrate the point:

- While Scripture says that faith is not a matter of what a person eats or drinks (Rom 14:17), one group of Christians might focus

---

4. See verses about "believe and be saved": John 1:12; 3:16; 18, 36; 6:40, 47; 11:25–26; 20:31; Acts 4:12; 16:30–31; Rom 10:9–10, 13; Eph 2:8–9; 1 John 5:13

PRINCIPLE 5 | HOW ARE JUDGMENT AND FREE WILL DANGEROUS GIFTS?

on following the Old Testament dietary laws. That is a nice thing, maybe a healthy thing to do, but it is not a salvation issue.

- While Scripture tells us that Jesus will be the one who baptizes believers with the Holy Spirit,[5] another group of Christians might declare that water baptism by immersion is required. Participating in water baptism is a wonderful testimony of our faith, but water baptism done to us by a person other than the Holy Spirit is not a salvation issue. (See Appendix I for more about water baptism versus baptism by the Holy Spirit.)

- While Scripture tells us that any day to worship God is the same as any other (Rom 14:5–6), another group of Christians might prefer to worship on a particular day of the week. It is good to worship God every day. Picking one specific day is a nice thing to do, but which one we select does not affect our salvation.

- While Scripture tells us that dancing can be an act of worship[6] and that Jesus drank and even made wine,[7] another group of Christians might insist that Christians are not allowed to dance or drink alcohol. Disciplines that help people live away from the world or control addictions are a helpful thing to do, but those rules are not a requirement of salvation.

Many denominations of Christianity have been formed because their followers are strengthened in their faith when they focus on those things. There is nothing unchristian about a group of people following those doctrines in an effort to express their love for Jesus. On the other hand, there is nothing more Christian about a group of people who follow those doctrines than a group who doesn't. The danger is not so much about having a focus or suggesting rules of conduct. The danger is in setting out a list of things a person must do or not do in order to be a "Christian" and thus be saved. It is easy for such a focus to become an attempt to gain salvation through works. It says, "Do these things and God will find you acceptable; don't do them and you aren't really a Christian."

That would be judging the hearts of others and deciding whether or not they are actually true believers. It would be us tagging "traditions" onto what the one thing Jesus said to do—believe. It would bring us closer to

---

5. Matt 3:11; Luke 3: 15–18; John 1:31–34; Acts 1:5
6. Ps 149:3; 150:4; 2 Sam 6:14
7. Luke 7:33–34; John 2

becoming modern-day Pharisees. Jesus called the Pharisees in his day "a brood of vipers" (snakes). Ouch. Do we want him to look at us that way?

Paul specifically confirms that is it is fine to hold on to activities or biblical beliefs which help us grow our faith. In the same breath, however, Paul cautions us not to judge other people's faith or what they do in order to express that faith. Judging non-salvation issues may make other believers stumble in their faith. Those believers may second guess themselves. They may worry over not doing enough. Or doing too much. Or not doing something right.

> Therefore let us stop passing judgment on one another. Instead, make up your mind not to put any stumbling block or obstacle in the way of a brother or sister (Rom 14:13).

Doing or not doing certain activities as part of a person's faith are examples of God's permissive will. If we think one of them is important for us to do or not do, God is evidently fine with it, because he knows our hearts, and knows those things are a way we are expressing our love for him. They are permitted, as long as underneath it all, we have the basic requirement for salvation: belief in Jesus.

What was that basic requirement for salvation again? Belief in Jesus. Not anything we do to express our faith.

We are, as always, to leave judgment of the heart—where our faith resides with the Holy Spirit—to God. And as God's church, we are to get along; we are to have grace for each other in things that are nonessentials in our faith.

> Accept the one whose faith is weak, without quarreling over disputable matters (Rom 14:1)

Paul then summarizes what we should do.

> So whatever you believe about these things keep between yourself and God (Rom 14:22).

God doesn't want us to argue about preferential doctrine unrelated to salvation. Other believers are following a preferential doctrine out of their love of Christ. Our own faith should be centered on our relationship between us and God.

Connection Point: Have you ever felt another Christian was judging your faith? Have you ever been guilty of judging theirs?

How can you remember to focus only on what Christians have in common instead of participating in disagreements over issues that are not a requirement for salvation?

Chapter Summary

- **Theology Simplified:** We are to apply God's gift of discernment to the actions of unbelievers, other believers, ourselves, and scripturally based teachings, making sure not to argue about church disciplines unrelated to salvation. Our own faith should be centered on our relationship between us and God.

- **What's it to me?** It's tough to see the super fine line between all that great discernment you have and judging people's hearts. Learning how God has loved you though and learning how to love others helps you get over that. Learning to trust God more helps you release people you want to judge into God's hands. He will take care of their souls so you don't have to ever think about it again. And he will do it right.

- **Faith Simplified:** We are to discern the actions of others but leave judgment to God.

16

Free Will

What is free will?

GOD GAVE US INTELLIGENCE and an ability to gain knowledge and experience that allows us to be discerning. God further gave us the ability to make choices based on that intelligence, knowledge, experience, and discernment. God does not dictate every aspect of our lives. Rather, he allows us to make choices at every moment of every day. The ability to make choices is God's gift of free will.

We have touched on the issue of free will several times in this book. We see the first exercise of free will back in the Garden of Eden. Although God instructed Adam and Eve not to eat the fruit from the Tree of Knowledge of Good and Evil, they did anyway. They used their free will to make the choice to disobey God.

As God often does, he accomplished several good things because, and in spite of, Adam and Eve's disobedience. By eating the forbidden fruit, mankind received the knowledge of good and evil right at the time it was needed most—when Adam and Eve left the Garden to live in a world ruled by Satan. God even made leaving the Garden itself a good thing. Leaving, meant mankind could no longer live forever. Dying thus gave us (our souls) the opportunity to ultimately be in the presence of God the Father, in Heaven, freed from our physical bodies. Of course, we have to exercise our free will and choose to do so—by accepting Jesus' gift of salvation.

Eternity aside, God has given us leniency in how to live our earthly lives. God gave us the Ten Commandments as guidelines for us to live well.

We have the free will to either live by those laws or ignore them; just as we have the free will to live according to the laws of society or ignore them. The point with free will is that we will have consequences for whatever choice we make—even if those choices are not inherently "sinful." Those consequences can be bad or good.

> **To illustrate the point:** George chose a job that offered worldly advancement, wealth, and financial security. George's job is not sinful and George's worldly job offers opportunities to love others in God's name as he interacts with co-workers and clients.
>
> The consequences of his worldly job, however, have meant that George has less time with family, more stress, a focus on things of the world and less on God—all of which affect George's own well-being and his relationships with family and friends who want his time and attention. Those are consequences of George's non-sinful choice.
>
> George chooses to exercise each day and as a consequence he has more energy and sleeps better. George's friend, Evelyn has chosen to eat bagels for breakfast every morning. As a consequence, Evelyn now has type 2 diabetes.
>
> Evelyn's non-sinful lifestyle choices also have consequences that affect others. Because Evelyn is now a diabetic, her family has to change their diet in order to accommodate Evelyn's poor health. Her doctor warns her that her diabetes has affected her foot and it will have to be amputated. Evelyn's husband now faces a future as Evelyn's main health care giver because of her poor choices.

Another consequence of bad choices is understanding the harm we have caused others—that sense of guilt and responsibility we will carry throughout our lives. When we live selfishly, we may turn others away from us to the point where they no longer want to be in our lives. If we one day recognize the hurt we have caused them, we may not be able to receive their forgiveness. Or they may forgive us at a spiritual level but have been too hurt to allow us back into their lives.

In other words, God has given us free will to make choices. The consequences of the choices we make may affect ourselves, others, our present situation, our relationships, our future, the world. Every choice we make has a consequence.

Free Will

Connection Point: What free will choices have you made in your life that led to consequences you wish you had avoided? What free will choices other people made have led to consequences that affected you personally? What have you had to do in order to help overcome the consequences of those choices?

The Narrow Road

Our journey to an eternal presence with God the Father in Heaven, starts by making the free will decision to believe in Jesus. Jesus referred to this journey to Heaven as walking the Narrow Road.

> "But small is the gate and narrow the road that leads to life, and only a few find it" (Matt 7:14).

That verse is coupled with

> Jesus answered, "I am the way and the truth and the life. No one comes to the Father except through me" (John 14:6).

Only the Narrow Road leads to eternal life with the Father. Jesus is that Narrow Road. Jesus is that way, set in motion as part of the Father's overall plan, which he created in the beginning. The Narrow Road was created for every person to take as the way to live eternally in his presence. We set foot on that Narrow Road by first going through the gate—accepting Jesus' gift of salvation.

Clearly, this Narrow Road is not a physical road, but a spiritual one. The spiritual road is big and wide enough to allow all people to walk it. But it is narrow in the sense that it is the only way to the Father.

For Greater Depth

> The Greek word used in Matthew 7:14 is *thlibo*. *Thlibo* is defined as made narrow.[1] Defining a word by using the same word isn't helpful in this case. So let's look at a definition of the English word *narrow* to see if that adds clarification. *Merriam Webster* lists a definition for *narrow* as limited in scope. Other dictionaries

1. Zodhiates, *Dictionary,* 736

> include the definition *restricted*.[2] That definition helps us better understand God's Narrow Road.

While God's Narrow Road is wide enough to allow all people who have ever and will ever live to reach him, the entrance to that road is restricted to those people who have made the free will choice to follow Jesus onto that road. Jesus, therefore, is the entrance (the gate) to that road, as well as the road (the way) itself.

Remember our subway turnstile illustration? At the subway station, we are all given a ticket. We each have the ability to drop our ticket into the turnstile slot. There are enough tickets for everyone. The tickets are free. Jesus paid for all of them himself. There is an endless number of subway trains going to Heaven. But we have to drop that ticket into the slot before we can go through the gate.

> **Connection Point**: What do you think about the fact that God's Narrow Road must go through Jesus? Do you think God is being unfair or unreasonable? Or do you see it as a way for God to offer salvation to all people?

Our perfect path along the Narrow Road

In addition to God's Narrow Road, he has individualized our path along that road in order for each of us to have a God-filled life.

> "Before I formed you in the womb I knew you, before you were born I set you apart" (Jer 1:5).

God also tells us,

> "For I know the plans I have for you," declares the Lord, "plans to prosper you and not to harm you, plans to give you hope and a future" (Jer 29:11).

Although God spoke those two verses to Jeremiah, they indicate truths for all of us. God formed each of us in the womb but knew us even before that. God has plans for each of us. That's right. God loves you specifically, so

---

2. Merriam-Webster, s.v. "narrow (adj.)"

Free Will

much that he made an individualized, personalized, custom-tailored plan just for you.

Because we know God's character, we know those plans are to give us hope and a future. The future which God has planned for us, is to spend eternity with him. The surety of hope we have is solid because God's plan of redemption has already been accomplished by Jesus. All we have to do is say "yes" to Jesus and step onto the Narrow Road with him. We do so by using our free will to make that choice.

Even if we are on the Narrow Road though; even if we recognize that God has individualized a path for us along that road, we continue to have free will. While on the Narrow Road, we may tell the Holy Spirit we don't need his guidance in a decision. Or we may decide to expand our path beyond what God desires. Or we may want to take a different route—which turns out to be filled with potholes and roadblocks.

What, then would a life that follows God's perfect, individualized path look like?

> **To illustrate the point:** Jesus, in the flesh, was still God. He could do whatever he wished. Jesus, as a human, had free will. As both a mortal man and God in the flesh, Jesus' individual free will was, at the same time, to do the will of the Father.[3]
>
> Jesus' perfect path then was basically a straight line. He was born in a manger in Bethlehem. His life was threatened by the King for the first years of his life. His family was forced to move to Egypt to escape death, later returning to Nazareth—where, according to Nathaniel, nothing good comes from (John 1:46). When Jesus began his ministry, the Pharisees and Sadducees hated him. He was abandoned by many of his followers. He was arrested, prosecuted unfairly. He was tortured and killed. That was Jesus' perfect path for his earthly life.
>
> Within that plan for Jesus' life, however, there were moments where he could have strayed from that path. Jesus could have answered the charges against him in a way that let him off the hook. He could have walked away from the impending crucifixion. He could have stepped down from the cross. But those things were not part of Jesus' perfect path. Jesus' perfect path— individualized for him and by him as God and designed by the

---

3. John 6:38; see other verses about doing the will of the Father: Matt 7:21; 12:50; 26:39; John 5:19, 30; 6:40

Father—led to his death on the cross. Jesus walked his perfect path.

Straying from our perfect path and returning to it

If you've read the book of Leviticus, you know it can be dry and tiresome. Fess up. Who has ever slid through reading Leviticus without actually reading every single word? That was the case for Jim. So at one point Jim prayed before he began reading Leviticus.

> Lord, you put the book of Leviticus in the Bible for a reason. Please show me what you want me to understand from this book. Amen.

As Jim read, he began to see a pattern.

- Do this, offer this sacrifice.
- Encounter this issue, do this.
- If this happens to you, make sure you respond this way.

It soon became clear. There is nothing you can do—no mistake you can make; no sin you can commit—that God doesn't have a way for you to return to him.

> **To illustrate the point:** Our Holy Bible is filled with mess-ups. Abraham basically prostituted his wife Sarah—twice. David was an adulterer and a murderer. While Moses was up on the mountain talking with God, Aaron led the people into crafting an idol of gold and worshipping it. Moses himself killed an Egyptian and escaped into the hills to avoid punishment. He also argued with God about leading the people, basically saying he didn't want to do it.
>
> But Abraham was declared righteous by God. Why?
> God referred to David as a man after his own heart. Why?
> God chose Aaron and his tribe of Levites as the priesthood who alone were allowed to come into God's presence, serve him, and have God himself as their inheritance. Why?
> Moses ultimately said "yes" to God and led millions of God's chosen people out of slavery. He also wrote out the body of laws so cherished by the Jewish people that it is still referred to as "The Law of Moses." Why?

Because God doesn't look at our past or our present. He looks at our heart. God clearly didn't give up on those people. God doesn't give up on us either.

> The Lord is not slow in keeping his promise, as some understand slowness. Instead he is patient with you, not wanting anyone to perish, but everyone to come to repentance (2 Pet 3:9).

In Jesus' parable of the prodigal son (Luke 15:11–32), a man's youngest son took his inheritance before his father had even died and went into the world to squander it. Then he returned to his father's home, repentant and sorrowful for what he had done. The father greeted him with joy and celebrated his return, reminding us of God's consistent character recorded in the book of Joel.

> "Even now," declares the Lord, "return to me with all your heart, with fasting and weeping and mourning." Rend your heart and not your garments. Return to the Lord your God, for he is gracious and compassionate, slow to anger, and abounding in love, and he relents from sending calamity (Joel 2:12–13).

Our Heavenly Father greets us with joy and celebrates when we return to him—and when we return to the perfect path he has created for our journey of faith.

Connection Point: Have you recognized God's perfect path for you? Have there been times when you returned to the path after straying from it? How has God's love for you after returning to the path given you confidence and trust in him for the rest of the journey?

To illustrate the point: The Apostle Paul also had a perfect path individualized for him. Paul was born into a Jewish family and was raised as a God-fearing Jew. He feared God so much that Paul (as Saul) became a Pharisee—focusing more on following God's law than on loving him.

That focus on strict legality took Paul away from God's perfect path for him. After Jesus' death and resurrection, Paul took to persecuting Christians and participating in their murder. Ultimately, as Paul was on the road to Damascus to hunt down and persecute more Christians, Jesus intervened. Jesus confronted

Paul, introduced himself to Paul as Savior, and provided Paul with a way to return to the perfect path he had individualized for Paul.

Even after Paul began to walk the Narrow Road with Jesus and follow the perfect individualized path for his life, however, Paul continued to stumble.

> I do not understand what I do. For what I want to do I do not do, but what I hate I do (Rom 7:15).

Each time Paul stumbled, God welcomed Paul when he returned to the perfect individualized path for his life.

God's plan for everyone is to walk the Narrow Road. God sent us Jesus to encourage us to choose that plan. The Father also created a perfect path for us along that Narrow Road. The perfect path, however, does not impact our salvation because when we accept Jesus' gift of salvation, we are sealed for eternity. Done deal.

We all sin, however, and sometimes we stray from the perfect path. God's individualized perfect path is there to encourage us to keep choosing him. The Holy Spirit can advise us how to follow the path. At the end of the day, however, we each must choose to take the path and stay on it. As always, free will is there for us to use.

Our perfect path includes works to do

God's individualized perfect path for each of us, includes specific works God has laid out for us to do. He has gifted us with spiritual gifts to benefit other believers and to reflect his goodness into the world. He has also gifted us with talents and abilities that enrich our days. He has placed people and opportunities in our lives.

Those works God has laid out for us are not for his benefit. God has everything he needs. If we do not do those works, God can do them himself or get someone else to do them. In fact, God's plan will still be perfect if no one ever does those works. Rather, those works are for our benefit. They are to enrich our lives; to bring us joy; to build relationships; to find fulfillment. They are to bring us closer to God as we seek his leading and honor him with what we do and how we live.

Nevertheless, one of the most troubling verses of Scripture for some Christians comes from the book of James.

> As the body without the spirit is dead, so faith without deeds is dead (Jas 2:26).

The Greek word used for spirit in this verse is *pneuma*. Earlier we saw that *pneuma* refers not to our soul and who we are, but rather to our ability to communicate with God's Holy Spirit. Thus, James reminds us of the importance of communion—and our relationship—with God.

In chapter 12, we discussed how all of us humans were given the ability to communicate with God—through our spirit. If we have not made the choice to believe in Jesus, our spirit has not connected with God's Spirit. Because we have not said "yes" to Jesus, when our body dies, our eternal soul does not live eternally in Heaven with the Father. James reminds us here that when our soul—the essence of who we are—is released from our physical body at death, that's it. There ain't no more.

Our body without our Holy Spirit-activated soul, is dead. We do not have eternal life in Heaven. We are separated forever and ever from God's presence. Without our spirit connected to the Holy Spirit, our bodies along with our souls (who we are) are dead forever.

We worry that James' *dead faith* means we are not saved. But clearly, Scripture tells us that we are not saved by anything we do ourselves (deeds). We are only saved by our faith in what Jesus has done for us. At that point, our souls are sealed forever by the Holy Spirit, because our spirit had connected to God's Spirit.

> For it is by grace you have been saved, through faith—and this is not from yourselves, it is the gift of God—not by works, so that no one can boast (Eph 2:8–9).

For Greater Depth

> The specific Greek word for *dead* used in James 2:26 to refer to faith without deeds is *nekros*. In this specific verse, dead means inactive, inoperable.[4]

James didn't say anything about salvation in that verse. If he had been suggesting we lose our salvation when we don't do deeds, he surely would have said so. Instead, based on the definition of the original Greek word,

4. Zodhiates, *Dictionary*, 1006–1007

nekros, James 2:26 infers that without deeds, a person's faith remains, but the person is not doing anything with it. A person's salvation is secure based on a belief in Jesus, but that faith is inoperative. The faith remains; but it is inactive; or rather, *we* are inactive in expressing that faith by doing something with it.

Let's return to Ephesians 2:8–9 that we have been saved by faith, not works. The very next verse says:

> For we are God's handiwork, created in Christ Jesus to do good works, which God prepared in advance for us to do (Eph 2:10).

We are saved by faith in grace given us by what Jesus did (Eph 2:8–9). Then, we are expected to do good works that God prepared for us to do (Eph 2:10). The verse about being saved is immediately followed by the verse about good works. They do not contradict each other. They complement each other.

But why does God want us to do good works?

> Our people must learn to devote themselves to doing what is good, in order to provide for urgent needs and not live unproductive lives (Titus 3:14).

> In the same way, let your light shine before others, that they may see your good deeds and glorify your Father in heaven (Matt 5:16).

These two verses tell us that our good works provide for the needs of others, building up the body of Christ and showing God's love through us in a way that allows others to recognize the value of our faith. Those good works do not earn us salvation. But they are evidence that our faith is alive and active. And our example of faith just might incline someone else to look into what Jesus has to offer.

Remember though, that those good works are not the evidence God looks for to prove our salvation. The only evidence of our faith God looks at resides in our heart—the presence of the Holy Spirit, given to us when we first put our faith in Jesus. Rather, good works, are evidence to the world. They are a way to show our love for God, to show our gratitude for what he has done for us, to honor him, and to spread his love into the world by what we do in his name. They are a powerful testimony to people who do not yet know Jesus.

While we do not lose or gain salvation based on whether we do those works, there are clear benefits for doing them. Using our God-given abilities makes our lives richer. Using our abilities for his purpose helps us draw closer to him. Drawing closer to God enriches our relationship with him. As we use our abilities to do things for others and live out our increasing depth of faith in God, our relationship with other people improves. The walk along the Narrow Road is simply better if we are more attuned to the leading of the Holy Spirit and doing what the Father has equipped us to do. God will want us to give an account of whether we chose to stay on the perfect path he created just for us or whether we used our free will and chose not to. But our salvation is secure either way.

If all we ever do is walk the Narrow Road with Jesus—never noticing or noticing but ignoring works which we sense God prepared for us to do—God's plan will still be beautiful and perfect. But our lives will be less joyful than they might be if we stayed on our individualized path. We are still on the Narrow Road with Jesus—but not taking the time to enjoy the path that takes us by a stream of still water that restores our soul. Or we miss the path that takes us up to the mountaintop where God is waiting to show us his glory. Or we miss the meadow where God wants to lead us to lie down in green pastures.

We often miss opportunities for benefit, joy, and relational growth—either because we say "no," because we ignore them intentionally, or because we simply do not recognize them. Sometimes, we even stray off our individualized perfect path on purpose. Fortunately, God always provides us with a way to return to our perfect path.

God has a plan. It is big and complex, and we can't see or understand all of it, but it is good, and we are part of it. The perfect path he has created for us is part of that plan. It is a different path for me than it is for you. But it is perfect because it is part of the Narrow Road Jesus walks with us. And God always provides a way for us to return to our perfect path, should we slip off the path by choices we make in life.

> **Connection Point**: Have you ever been troubled by James 2:26? Does this explanation give you confidence that although God wants you to do good works, they are not a requirement for salvation? Does this explanation of how Ephesians 2:8–9 and Ephesians 2:10 work together encourage you in your desire to work to honor God?

Chapter Summary

- **Theology Simplified:** God has a plan for all of humanity—to walk the Narrow Road to Heaven. God also has a plan for each of us individually. That individual perfect plan is intended to bring us joy, contentment, and deepen our relationship with the Father. We have to use our gift of free will to choose whether to say "yes" or "no" to both the Narrow Road and to our individual perfect path. God always welcomes us back if we should stray from that path.

- **What's it to me?** God has individualized a specific, unique, and wonderful plan for me? He sure has! It's your choice to follow that path, but since the path is part of Jesus' Narrow Road, it's got to be good, right? Who in your life might you like walking that Narrow Road with you and Jesus? How might you introduce them to Jesus so they are pointed in the right direction—the direction they make when they choose to say "yes" to Jesus?

- **Faith Simplified:** Good works don't assure our salvation but doing them can make our lives more satisfying and can deepen our relationship with God and others. Every choice has consequences; God's Narrow Road is open to everyone; he has a perfect path for each of us.

17

Our Most Important Free Will Choice

GOD THE FATHER ALLOWS us to make choices that affect our lives here on earth. Those choices have consequences—either for better or for worse. The most important choice we will ever make, however, is whether or not we freely accept Jesus' gift of salvation. The only way we can have eternal life in Heaven is by making that conscious, free will choice to say "yes."

Conversely, not making that free will choice is the only thing that will keep us out of Heaven. If we fail to make the choice, if we avoid making the decision, or if we postpone it until it is too late, in effect, we have said "no."

To illustrate the point: In computer programming, a software engineer creates default values. Often these defaults are the result of an if/then system. *If* the person using the computer presses "enter" on the keyboard, *then* a specific instruction is carried out. If the computer user presses any other key, nothing happens. The "nothing happens" is the default result of not pressing the "enter" key.

God, our spiritual software engineer, has designed a program of salvation. If we push the big red key, covered in stars and surrounded by blinking lights that says "yes," his instruction that we get eternal life with him is carried out.

If we press any other key on the keyboard—not just the "no" key, but any other key—nothing happens. The instruction that we get eternal life with God is not carried out. "Nothing happens/you don't go to Heaven" is the default result of not pressing the big red key.

The eternal consequence of our free-will *no* decision is that we have said "no" to Heaven and "yes" to eternity with Satan. God has given all of us eternal life. It is where we will spend eternity that is up to us.

Saying "yes" to Jesus allows us to step through the Narrow Gate and onto the Narrow Road that leads to eternal life with God the Father. Along that Narrow Road is our perfect path God has laid out for each of us, individualized to make the best use of the spiritual gifts, talents, and abilities God has equipped us with. Whether we detour from the path created for us or stay on it, is our free will choice. Whether to be on the road at all is our choice, too.

This is a short chapter to emphasize its importance. God's gift to us of free will is his most dangerous gift of all. The choice we make about his offer of salvation has eternal consequences. Very big eternal consequences.

> **Connection Point**: Did you think God would let everyone into Heaven regardless of whether or not they had said "yes" to Jesus? What is your thinking now? How does the fact that never saying "yes" means a person has in effect said "no" make you feel about the importance and urgency of responding?

Chapter Summary

- **Theology Simplified:** Free will is a gift that comes with enormous, eternal consequences. All other choices are insignificant compared with the choice given us by God the Father. The choice to say "yes" to Jesus results in eternity in Heaven. A choice to say "no" to Jesus results in eternity in Hell.

- **What's it to me?** If you have already said "yes" to Jesus, then you can see how wonderful God's gift really is. If you have been learning about Jesus, even following his teachings, but haven't said "yes" yet, you can see that "not getting around to making that choice" is actually saying "Thanks anyway, but I'll just skip the whole eternal, joy-filled, heavenly experience with you, God." If you have someone in your life who hasn't yet said "yes," this understanding might make you more passionate about sharing the importance of that decision with them.

- **Faith Simplified:** We have to say "yes" to Jesus in order to spend eternity in Heaven. That is the best choice with the best eternal consequences.

This is the fifth principle of *Faith Simplified*: judgment and free will are dangerous gifts.

18

Simplifying Our Faith

GOD THE FATHER HAS an immense, vast, enormous, massively complex, intricate, multifaceted, and elaborate plan that we don't fully understand. Our part in that plan, however, is simple. God has equipped us with rules to live by, abilities, and free will. God has also created an individualized perfect path for each of us. We have free will to follow that path or not. If we do, our lives will be better because we will grow closer to him. If we do not follow that path or if we stray from it, we do so with that same free will. But if we stray from that path, God always—not just sometimes or for some people, but always—provides a way to return to him, using our free will and choosing to do so. That perfect path, along Jesus' Narrow Road, leads straight to the Father and Heaven.

Our Heavenly Father began implementing the salvation part of his plan back when he first created the universe. He did so because he wants us to personally experience eternal life in his presence. His plan also includes the opportunity to know, love, and experience him while we are living this earthly life through our relationship with the Holy Spirit, made possible by Jesus. When we have a relationship with God and become an active participant in his plan, we receive benefits in this earthly life, such as:

- We have an eternal perspective that makes our troubles in this life feel temporary
- We can focus on God's power; not our own
- Struggles make our faith stronger as we lean in to God

- Our relationship with God becomes our first priority; relationships with others are second and both become richer
- Because salvation is God's free gift to us; faith means we then live to honor God and live in His presence (not to gain salvation)
- We get earthly rewards now, by sowing thankfulness, love, and gratitude, and harvesting the same in abundance
- God's plan is not for us to be isolated but to share and be in community with others
- Relationships with others strengthen our faith journey as we mentor, teach, and keep each other accountable
- Others see Christ through us and vice versa

In this book we have looked at five principles of Christianity:

- We can trust God's plan
- We need a Savior
- God's rules are for our benefit
- Jesus fulfilled the law by providing all we need for salvation
- Judgment and free will are gifts with dangerous consequences

After studying the principles, we understand better why we should trust God's plan. We recognize our need for a Savior who would provide the blood sacrifice to not only cover our sins, but to forgive them completely. We appreciate how God gave us rules to make our lives better and bring us closer to him. We are grateful that Jesus further simplified those rules into two, reminding us that we are to love God and love others in every way we can and with everything we are.

God gave us an enormous gift when he relieved us from the burden of worrying over how God will judge us. We know that salvation is not about works we do on earth, but whether the Holy Spirit is living in our hearts, having sealed our souls for eternity. In this life, we can remember that we are simply to be discerning about the actions of others, and use that discernment to protect ourselves and others, to lift up believers, and to maintain and grow our own faith.

Moreover, we no longer have the burden to judge others. Of course we never had that burden in the first place. Still, many of us carried the perceived need to judge others around with us, dusting it off from time to time and hefting it on our backs. Recognizing we don't have that duty allows us to take the burden off our shoulders and throw it as far away from us as we can. The power of the Holy Spirit in us means he will multiply our strength with his when we do the throwing.

God's gift of free will allows us to make decisions in our life. Each decision has consequences—some good and some bad. The most important decision we will ever make is whether to accept Jesus' gift of eternal life in Heaven.

A greater understanding of Christian beliefs can deepen our faith as we see where those beliefs came from and as we believe them personally. That understanding can then help us as we share our faith with people who do not yet know Jesus, by giving us a deeper knowledge to help us answer their questions and explain why we believe what we do.

> **To illustrate the point:** Imagine talking with a friend who does not know Jesus. You share your personal testimony with your friend—what life was like before Jesus, how you came to say "yes" to Jesus, and how your life has been different since then.
>
> You continue, stating that Jesus died to be the sacrifice for our sins. Your friend looks blank but asks, "What do you mean? Why did Jesus have to die at all? How does his dying have anything to do with me?"
>
> You return the blank look and simply say, "Well, the Bible says so."
>
> Your friend has never read the Bible and has no reason yet to believe what it says. Your answer therefore does nothing to answer your friend's question. In fact, all it really does is make your argument in favor of Christianity look feeble and helpless.

That conversation has done nothing to help your friend understand Jesus' offer of salvation in a way that encourages your friend to accept his offer. This book addressed those questions your friend has. You may have had those same questions yourself before you became a believer in Jesus; or when you began reading this book. You now have greater understanding of what God's plan is and your place in it. Your confidence, based on your knowledge of what you believe and why, shows through in your response to your friend.

You answer your friend with the *what*, the *why*, and the *how* of salvation.

What?

I believe there is a God and he is trustworthy. He created everything around us. I believe the Bible is more than a historical book, but within its historical record, the Bible records how God has proven his trustworthiness with hundreds of examples, explaining what he promised and fulfilled throughout time. I believe God continues to prove his trustworthiness today. The greatest promise God made and fulfilled was to create a way for us to live eternally in Heaven with him. The way he completed that promise is through his Son, Jesus' sacrificial death on the cross.

Why?

God loves you so much that he created this entire universe for you to be in and created a detailed plan for you personally. But if you observe the world, you can see that God's creation—mankind—has fallen from its original perfection. We disobey God. We pay no attention to him. Sometimes, we do not even acknowledge his existence. Those are all things God does not desire for us in order to live a good life. Those acts of disobedience are sins against him that need to be forgiven in order to be in a right relationship with him. As unforgiven, imperfect people, we cannot enter perfect, holy Heaven.

How?

Despite our imperfection and tendency to sin, God still loves us. He therefore sent a Savior so that each of us can be forgiven and made acceptable to the Father. This forgiveness allows the Father to see us through his holy and sinless eyes. Being forgiven and made right with God allows us to have eternal life in Heaven with the Father. That Savior—the one who provided a way for us to be forgiven—is Jesus Christ. Jesus' salvation is for you personally.

What/why/how?

Throughout history, people have sacrificed animals as an offering to God to spiritually cover their sins and be made acceptable to God. Because divine Jesus was fully worthy, only his blood sacrifice which he freely gave was sufficient to not just cover our sins, but to forgive them, restoring our relationship with the Father for all time and making it possible for the Holy Spirit to live within us. At our physical death, the Holy Spirit in us testifies that our soul—the eternal being we are—belongs to Jesus. Our eternity in perfect Heaven is assured.

Now

God the Father also gave us the gift of free will. That gift has a cost—you must consciously make the decision to accept salvation through Jesus. That decision is about choosing your own destiny. It is the single most important decision you will ever make in your life.

By explaining these steps, you show your friend that Christianity is for thinking people who choose Christianity because it is the logical thing to do. To help you further see the reasoning and simplicity of our part in God's plan, the Apostle Paul set it all out step-by-step in the book of Romans. Those steps are sometimes called the *Roman Road to Salvation*. (See Appendix J for the steps described in the book of Romans.)

Underneath, within, and woven through all of these principles, is the working of God's gift of free will. In all things, God has given us choice. We have a choice to participate actively in God's plan. We have a choice to live by God's rules. We have a choice to love or not love God or other people. We recognize, however, that every choice comes with a consequence. The most important choice we have to make is where we will spend eternity. But God made even that choice simple for us: either say "yes" or "no" to Jesus' offer of salvation. Say "yes" and you have chosen to be with God in Heaven forever. Say "no" or say nothing and you have chosen Hell.

We saw how throughout Scripture God chose us before the creation of the world to be part of his family (Eph 1:4). God *chose us*. God chose and planned and predestined all of mankind and each of us individually, *intending* us to be with him eternally in Heaven.

For Greater Depth

> The Greek word for *chosen* in Ephesians 1:4 is *eklego*. In that specific verse, it includes the reasoning that God chose us for himself out of kindness, favor, and love.[1] *Predestined* as used in

---

1. Zodhiates, *Dictionary*, 544

> Ephesians 1:11 and Romans 8:29, is the Greek word *proorizo*.[2] It means to determine or decree beforehand. *Proorizo* specifically refers to God's determination beforehand about the benefits of salvation, the actions he would take in order to accomplish that plan, and how each of us would have to react in order to gain salvation ourselves.

God doesn't direct our every thought. God didn't decide ahead of time every action we take in life. He didn't decide ahead of time which of us would say "yes" to Jesus' offer. Rather he chose all of us to be eligible to be part of his plan. He predestined (decided; determined; decreed) the details of his plan. He predestined (decided; determined; decreed) how he would implement that plan. He predestined (decided; determined; decreed) that mankind would have the ability to choose to be part of his plan. He predestined (decided; determined; decreed) mankind to be an active and important part of his plan, if we individually choose to be.

God chose us to be part of his eternal plan. But we have to choose him in return. We have to say "yes" to his plan by exercising the free will he gave us to do so. Saying "yes" is us agreeing to God's offer. A covenant is created. Because we understand God's character, we know He will keep that covenant. He always does.

In fact, all of the deep, meticulous, and intricately detailed theology that has ever existed within Christianity comes down to one thing: in order to live eternally with God the Father in Heaven, we must exercise our free will and choose to accept his free gift of salvation through Jesus.

God did everything for us. He created the plan. He gave us knowledge, wisdom, discernment, and minds to make good decisions. He even sacrificed his own Son, Jesus to provide the way for us to be part of the plan. God did it all, leaving only one thing left for us to gain eternal life: say "yes."

If you have given your heart to Jesus, the Holy Spirit is within you right now. Your salvation is guaranteed. Saved forever! If you haven't, remember that the default to not saying "yes" is "no;" even if you *intended to say "yes" but just never got around to it*.

We can only glimpse the complexities of God's plan. He has filled our lives and future with blessings we can barely take in. He loves us with a love

---

2. Zodhiates, *Dictionary*, 1223–1224

beyond what we can imagine. And he has presented all of it to us lavishly, resplendent, arranged on a magnificent tray, gilded with gold and dotted with dazzling jewels. "All this is for you," he says. "Will you accept my gifts?"

It's not a trick question. There is no "catch." All we have to do is say "yes" and everything is ours. We become his children. We join God's family. We receive his inheritance, including residence in his eternal home, in his holy presence. There we are protected forever from evil, sorrow, pain, and death.

If we say "no," we are saying "no" to eternal life in Heaven. If we say "no," we are saying "yes" to eternity in Hell. God's default consequence if we do not say "yes" is that we have said "no." If we say, "I'll think about it," but never get around to saying "yes," we have said "no" because we never said "yes." We must make a conscious choice to say "yes." Based on knowledge, understanding, wisdom, and discernment, using the abilities God has given us, the most rational, reasonable, logical, sensible, obvious, and appropriate answer is "yes."

As for me, it's not just a matter of saying "yes." It's a matter of saying "Of course! You bet! I sure will! Absolutely! Definitely! Unequivocally! By all means!"

It really is that simple.

Chapter Summary

- **Theology Simplified:** God's plan is revealed in detail throughout Scripture, all the way from the beginning of Creation to well past Jesus' death and resurrection. Basically, it's this: God has a plan for us to live forever in Heaven. The only way we can do so is by accepting Jesus' offer of salvation made possible when he provided the only blood sacrifice sufficient to make us acceptable enough to be in the Father's presence. Everything has been done for us, with the one tiny exception. We have to say "yes."

- **What's it to me?** You have seen how God's plan is recorded and revealed in Scripture starting way back at the beginning. You have learned a bit about theology, enough to make some sense of Christian beliefs. You have then set those big words and complicated concepts up on your spiritual shelf. Meanwhile, your faith can grow stronger because you now know what Christians believe and why. And because you know, you can fully embrace those beliefs and fully believe them, too. And then share them with others.

- **Faith Simplified:** God so loved the world…including you. Saying "yes" to Jesus' offer is a choice with the very best consequence of all: Heaven. Once you understand what this gift of salvation means, you are now prepared to "give an answer to everyone who asks you to give the reason for the hope that you have" (1 Pet 3:15). Did you say "yes"? Are you prepared to tell others about Jesus?

This is our prayer for you.

> Heavenly Father, thank you for including us in your plan and for loving us enough to want to share perfect Heaven with us imperfect people. Thank you for sending Jesus to satisfy your requirements of sacrifice so we can be forgiven and brought into a loving relationship with you. Thank you for choosing us in the beginning and for giving us the opportunity to choose you in return.
>
> Please work in our minds and hearts, Holy Spirit, to help us better understand our place in your plan, to deepen our faith, and give us confidence to powerfully share your offer of salvation with others. We pray all of this in Jesus' name. Amen.

Appendix A

The Apostles' Creed

The Apostles' Creed is a summary of the teachings of the original Apostles—those disciples who lived and learned at Jesus' feet. The creed was formalized in 140 AD—fairly soon after Jesus' death and resurrection in terms of church history. The importance of that early date is there was little time for individual ideas to crop up that weren't part of Jesus' teaching. *The Apostles' Creed* thus remains true to what Jesus taught to his chosen disciples. Here is the creed.

> I believe in God, the Father almighty,
> creator of heaven and earth.
> I believe in Jesus Christ, his only Son, our Lord.
> He was conceived by the power of the Holy Spirit
> and born of the virgin Mary.
> He suffered under Pontius Pilate,
> was crucified, died, and was buried.
> He descended to the dead.
> On the third day he rose again.
> He ascended into heaven,
> and is seated at the right hand of the Father.
> He will come again to judge the living and the dead.
> I believe in the Holy Spirit,
> the holy catholic Church,
> the communion of the saints,
> the forgiveness of sins,
> the resurrection of the body,
> and the life everlasting. Amen.

Note that the term *holy catholic church* here does not refer to the Roman Catholic Church. Rather, the meaning of *catholic* here is universal, unlimited, world-wide. *The Apostles' Creed* nicely summarizes Christian theology—what all mainstream Christian denominations have in common—nothing added; nothing taken away.

Appendix B

Discussion of *Praus* (*Meek*) in Horse Training

CHAPTER 1 USES THE illustration of a small girl stroking the nose of a massive horse as an example of the definition of *praus* (*meek*) as gentleness in power. There is some discussion among Bible scholars, about whether the term *praus* was historically used in horse training by the Greek army. While that discussion is of limited importance when understanding the ancient Greek word, for the reader interested in digging deeper, the following sources discuss the horse training connection or further define the original Greek word *praus* related to horses. See the Bibliography for detailed source information.

- Mounce, William D., *Complete Expository Dictionary of Old and New Testament Words*.
- Mounce, William D., Robert H. Mounce, *The Zondervan Greek and English Interlinear New Testament (NASB/NIV)*. This resources uses the Goodrich/Kohlenberger numbering system, code 4558.
- Elwell, Walter A., ed., *Evangelical Dictionary of Theology*.
- The use of the word *praus* relating to horses is also suggested by the writings of Athenian military leader and historian Xenophon (c. 430-354 BC) in his writings *On Horsemanship* and *The Art of Horsemanship*.

Appendix C

God's Plan

Let's flesh out those 4-point bullets of God's plan we looked at in Chapter 2.

- After God created everything, he gave us knowledge of good and evil to prepare us to live in a world filled with evil. He then made us mortal—the first step for our souls to spend eternity with the Father. He also instituted the sacrificial system to cover our sins by sacrificing one of his own creatures.
- Several thousands of years lapsed between Creation and the next step. God saved a remnant of humanity to rebuild mankind based on Noah—the one man who trusted him.
- Several hundred years later, God selected Abraham through whom he would implement his salvation plan.
- Abraham's grandson Jacob, renamed Israel by God, went to live in Egypt during a famine, where his son Joseph was in charge of Egypt's food supply.
- Israel's family lived in Egypt for several hundred years. Israel had 12 sons. Ten of those sons (not including Ruben and Joseph) and adding Joseph's two sons became known as the 12 tribes of Israel.
- While in Egypt, Israel's family grew into several million people.
- Joseph's high position in Egypt was forgotten over time. The Israelites were made slaves and treated harshly.

God's Plan

- Moses led Israel's family of millions out of Egypt and into the wilderness, transcribing God's laws into written form
- Joshua took Israel's family into the Promised Land, creating a nation, and dividing up that land among the 12 tribes.
- Several thousand years passed during which the Israelites alternated between following God and abandoning their faith in him.
- Jesus was born in Israelite society into the tribe of Judah. Jesus taught that he was the Son of God and that eternal life was possible only through him. He became the single blood sacrifice to make us acceptable to join the Father in Heaven forever.
- Our part in God's plan is to accept his offer of salvation through Jesus' sacrifice and receive eternal life in Heaven.
- Over 2,000 years have passed since Jesus' death, burial, and resurrection.
- God's plan of salvation is now and forever available to all people.
- We still have to say "yes" to God's offer for salvation.

Appendix D

God's Promises

ESTIMATES OF THE NUMBER of God's promises in Scripture vary depending on how they are counted. Here are some references if you'd like to see how certain scholars count them.

- 365 promises: See https://www.365promises.com
- 3000 promises: Forward Ministries. https://www.clintbyars.com/blog/2017/12/12/browse-a-list-of-gods-promises-from-each-book-of-the-bible.
- 3573 promises: Bibleinfo.com. https://www.bibleinfo.com/en/questions/how-many-bible-promises-are-there.
- 5467 promise: BibleGateway.com https://www.biblegateway.com/resources/dictionary-of-bible-themes/5467-promises-divine
- 7000 promises: OnePlace.com. Daily Hope with Rick Warren. https://www.oneplace.com/ministries/daily-hope/read/devotionals/daily-hope-with-rick-warren/praying-gods-promises-daily-hope-with-rick-warren-april-17-2018-11796629.html.
- 8810 promises: from paper written by Victor Knowles for Pepperdine University: Knowles, Victor (1998) "Promise and Fulfillment: Believing the Promises of God," Leaven: Vol. 6 : Iss. 3, Article 4. Available at: https://digitalcommons.pepperdine.edu/leaven/vol6/iss3/4.

Appendix E

Do People Go to Heaven if They Have Never Heard About Jesus?

WE KNOW THAT JESUS is "the way" to the Father. Belief in Jesus is what secures our salvation and provides our ticket to Heaven. But what about people who die never knowing what Jesus did? Do they get to go to Heaven, we wonder? Presented with the amazing truth of what Jesus did for everyone, including them, it's a good guess most people would choose to say "yes" if they had been given that offer in their lifetime.

Christian belief is that people in Old Testament times have been saved because they "died in faith." In other words, they died believing in God's promises even though they never knew what Jesus planned to do in the future (see Heb 11: 13–16). By extension, that belief hints that God would not abandon any soul without first giving them a way to make that important choice.

> The Lord is not slow in keeping his promise, as some understand slowness. Instead he is patient with you, not wanting anyone to perish, but everyone to come to repentance (2 Pet 3:9).

Peter reminds us that God wants everyone to repent. God wants none of his human creations to perish, but to join him in Heaven. Did God create a mechanism for salvation of people, whether they have ever officially heard of Jesus in this mortal lifetime? We have no Scripture that specifically confirms that idea. Therefore, that question is something we must put into our trust bucket for God to deal with. Our part of salvation is simply to say

Do People Go to Heaven if They Have Never Heard About Jesus?

"yes" to secure our own souls and to provide information, understanding, and testimony to encourage others to say "yes."

Appendix F

Why Did God Select the Levites as Priests?

WHILE IN THE DESERT, God appointed Aaron and Aaron's sons as his priests who would perform the religious duties on behalf of the Israelites. In fact, God decreed that anyone else who even approached the sanctuary was to be put to death (Num 3:10; see also Exod 28:1–4).

Aaron (and Moses, his brother) were both from the tribe of Levi. When God officially instituted the Levitical priesthood, he added all of the men from the entire tribe of Levi to serve as priests along with Aaron. Although Aaron was involved in the creation of the golden idol, other members of the tribe of Levi did not participate in worshipping the idol.

Moses had returned to camp from his time on the mountain with God and saw that the people were running wild and that Aaron had let them get out of control, worshipping the golden idol. When Moses stood at the entrance to the camp and said, "Whoever is for the Lord, come to me," all the Levites rallied to him. At Moses' instruction, the tribe of Levi then punished the other Israelites, killing 3,000 of the people who had worshipped the idol.

Afterwards Moses said, "You have been set apart to the Lord today, for you were against your own sons and brothers, and he has blessed you this day" (Exod 32:25–26, 29).

Because they upheld the holiness of God by not worshipping the idol and by "cleansing" the camp of people who had worshipped it, God chose the tribe of Levi to be his priesthood. This institution of the Levitical priesthood substituted Levite priests in place of the firstborn male for each family and did away with disorganized priestly selection. Instead of every firstborn male being consecrated (set apart) in service to the Lord, now only the tribe of Levites would serve him.

Appendix G

Works v. Grace

We know we can't work our way to Heaven by helping the poor, giving to charity, or serving in a homeless shelter. All of those things are good to do as evidence of our faith, but we are not saved by doing them. Similarly, we can't get to heaven simply by following God's laws. The legalistic Pharisees in Jesus' day focused on doing that. Trying to become righteous by following laws is another way people try to work to gain salvation by what they do rather than by relying on what Jesus already did on our behalf.

There are many verses of Scripture that talk about working for salvation, by following God's law versus God granting us salvation through grace (what we don't deserve) based on what Jesus did. Here are two verses where Paul explains how the law was useful to identify sin, but not to assure our salvation.

> Therefore no one will be declared righteous in God's sight by the works of the law [by working to follow the laws]; rather, through the law we become conscious of our sin (Rom 3:20, explanation added).

> So the law was our guardian until Christ came that we might be justified by faith. Now that this faith has come, we are no longer under a guardian (Gal 3: 24–25).

God gave the Israelites the law as a standard to help identify and define sin. Over time, the Pharisees had raised the standard of righteousness beyond what God had set out. By Jesus' time, the Pharisees' standard was so high, the Israelites kept trying and failing to achieve it. Thus, trying to obey the law effectively proved to mankind that we can never be righteous by what we do. Recognizing our inability to achieve God's standard on our own though, prepared us to accept Jesus' gift of salvation. We are saved not by working hard to obey; but through God's grace and forgiveness.

God's plan is simple. He commands us to be righteous. We can't be righteous on our own, so God makes us right with him (righteous) *by what he did for us*—through Jesus' sacrifice. When God the Father sent Jesus, He was doing something new. Something unheard of. Something simple for us.

Appendix H

Blasphemy

> And so I tell you, every kind of sin and slander can be forgiven,
> but blasphemy against the Spirit will not be forgiven
> (Matt 12:31–32, see also Mark 3:28–29; Luke 12:10).

WHAT DOES BLASPHEMY MEAN? The Greek word *blasphemeo* for *blasphemy* in Mark 3:28–29 and Luke 12:10 is defined as reviling against the Holy Spirit; to resist the conviction power of the Holy Spirit unto repentance. Similarly, the Greek word used in Matthew 12:31, *blasphemia*, means resistance against the convicting power of the Holy Spirit. (See Zodhiates, *Dictionary*, 340–341.)

When a person accepts Jesus' gift of salvation, he receives the Holy Spirit. It is the Holy Spirit that teaches, leads, and convicts a person of their sin. When a person rejects the Holy Spirit by saying "no" to Jesus, he has also said "no" to having the Holy Spirit living in him. That person has therefore said "no" to the Holy Spirit's power to convict that person of sin, and as a result, has rejected *the opportunity to ask for forgiveness.*

Here's the key: Jesus promised to forgive our sins if we ask. If we do not ask for forgiveness, Jesus does not forgive them. That's the way forgiveness of sin works. Forgiveness is freely given, but you have to ask for it first. If you don't have the Holy Spirit, you may not understand that you have sinned in the first place and you don't think you need forgiveness. So you don't ask for it.

Blasphemy

Blasphemy is not unforgivable simply because it is bad, although it is. All sins people commit are bad. Jesus forgives all of them if the person asks for forgiveness. Blasphemy is unforgivable because a person does not ask for forgiveness in the first place.

Don't ask for forgiveness; don't receive it. The sin remains unforgivable because it is unforgiven. It is unforgiven by a person's free will choice to say "no" to forgiveness, by saying "no" to Jesus and the Holy Spirit.

Appendix I

Baptism

WATER BAPTISM BEGAN IN the Old Testament. At that time water was used to purify people when they had become "unclean" due to disobedience to the laws of Moses. Only later was baptism related to repentance, as seen throughout John the Baptist's ministry. It was this repentance type of baptism that helped John prepare the way for Jesus.

Although Jesus underwent water baptism by John the Baptist and John's disciples, Jesus himself did not baptize people with water. Rather, Jesus said he would baptize with the Holy Spirit (Acts 11:15–16). Matthew and Luke record John the Baptist's words that he, John, baptized in water for repentance but Jesus would baptize with the Spirit and fire.

When the early church received the Holy Spirit, Scripture tells us that "what seemed to be tongues of fire" appeared over each of their heads (Acts 2:1–4). First Thessalonians 5:19 talks about not limiting the power of the Holy Spirit saying, *Do not quench the Spirit*. The original Greek word for *quench* here is *sbennumi*. It means to put out or extinguish a fire; also to figuratively dampen, hinder or repress. (See Zodhiates, *Dictionary*, 1282–83.)

John the Baptist knew there was an obvious connection between baptism by the Spirit and by fire. He knew that only Jesus had the power to do that kind of baptism. So John focused on water baptism of repentance. It is Jesus, however, who baptizes with the Holy Spirit (and fire). Although people in the early church often participated in water baptism as they do now, like it was for John the Baptist, baptism is an indication of faith and a symbolic showing of repentance to God.

Baptism

Water baptism (especially immersion baptism) is a big deal for many Christians. Is water baptism required or not? The people on the "no" side point to the people in Scripture who died before they could be baptized. The thief on the cross, for example, professed his faith in Jesus and Jesus told him he was saved. The thief had no opportunity to be baptized with water. The people on the "yes" side quote Jesus remark to "believe and be baptized."

Would God allow someone into Heaven who had said "yes" to Jesus, even if he had not been baptized? When Jesus added "be baptized," was he requiring believers to be immersed in water or did he mean that once we believed, the Holy Spirit would do the baptizing? What do you think?

Appendix J

The Roman Road to Salvation

PAUL NEATLY SET OUT five steps to salvation for us in the book of Romans. The steps are sometimes called *The Roman Road to Salvation*. Here they are.

1. Three separate verses describe the first step—recognizing our sinful nature.

    There is no one righteous, not even one (Romans 3:10).

    All have sinned and fallen short of the glory of God (Romans 3:23).

    The wages of sin is death (Romans 6:23).

2. Three verses describe what Jesus offers.

    But the gift of God is eternal life in Christ Jesus our Lord (Romans 6:23).

    But God demonstrates his own love for us in this: While we were still sinners, Christ died for us (Romans 5:8).

    Whoever calls on the name of the Lord will be saved (Romans 5:10).

3. Two verses state the steps to take.

    If you declare with your mouth, "Jesus is Lord," and believe in your heart that God raised him from the dead, you will be saved. For it is with your heart that you believe and are justified, and it is with your mouth that you profess your faith and are saved (Romans 10:9-10).

For, everyone who calls on the name of the Lord will be saved (Romans 10:13).

4. As a result, we have peace with God in this life.

   Therefore, since we have been justified through faith, we have peace with God through our Lord Jesus Christ, through whom we have gained access by faith into this grace in which we now stand (Romans 5:1–2).

5. Therefore, at judgment we will not be condemned. The consequence of not being condemned is everlasting life (referring back to step 2 and Jesus' offer of eternal life).

   Therefore, there is now no condemnation for those who are in Christ Jesus (Romans 8:1).

Bibliography

Arizona Christian University, Cultural Research Center. *American Worldview Inventory 2020 Results*. October 6, 2020. https://www.arizonachristian.edu/wp-content/uploads/2020/10/CRC_AWVI2020_Release11_Digital_04_20201006.pdf.

Baker, Warren, DRE, and Eugene Carpenter, PhD, eds. *Complete Word Study Dictionary Old Testament*. Chattanooga: AMG, 2003.

Baker, Warren, DRE, Tim Rake, and David Kemp, eds. *Complete Word Study Old Testament, King James Version*. Chattanooga: AMG, 1994.

Comfort, Philip W., and Walter A. Elwell, PhD, eds. *Tyndale Bible Dictionary*. Carol Stream: Tyndale, 2001.

Elwell, Walter A., ed., *Evangelical Dictionary of Theology*, Grand Rapids: Baker Academic, 2001.

King James Dictionary, biblestudytools.com. Accessed April 28, 2022. https://www.biblestudytools.com/dictionaries/king-james-dictionary.

Ligonier Ministries. *Highlights of 2020 State of Theology Survey*. September 26, 2020. https://www.ligonier.org/posts/theology-only-pastors.

———. *White Paper 2020 Lifeway Research Survey*. September 2020. http://research.lifeway.com/wp-content/uploads/2020/09/Ligonier-State-of-Theology-2020-White-Paper.pdf.

Merriam-Webster online dictionary. Accessed April 28, 2022. http://www.Merriam-Webster.com.

Mounce, William D., *Complete Expository Dictionary of Old and New Testament Words*. Grand Rapids: Zondervan Academic, 2006.

Mounce, William D., and Robert H. Mounce, *Zondervan Greek and English Interlinear New Testament (NASB/NIV)*. Grand Rapids: Zondervan, 2011.

Vine, W. E., Merrill F. Unger, and William White, Jr., eds. *Vine's Complete Expository Dictionary*. Nashville: Thomas Nelson, 1996.

Xenophon, and Henry Graham Dakyns, trans., *On Horsemanship*. N.p.: SMK Books, 2018.

Xenophon, and Morris H. Morgan, trans., *Art of Horsemanship*. Mineola, NY: Dover, 2006.

Zodhiates, Spiros, ThD, Warren Baker, DRE, Rev. George Hadjiantoniou, PhD, and Mark Oshman, ThM, eds. *Complete Word Study Dictionary New Testament*. Chattanooga: AMG, 1993.

Zodhiates, Spiros, ThD, Warren Baker, DRE, and Rev. George Hadjiantoniou, PhD, eds. *Complete Word Study Old Testament, King James Version*. Chattanooga: AMG, 1992.

www.ingramcontent.com/pod-product-compliance
Lightning Source LLC
Chambersburg PA
CBHW062023220426
43662CB00010B/1448